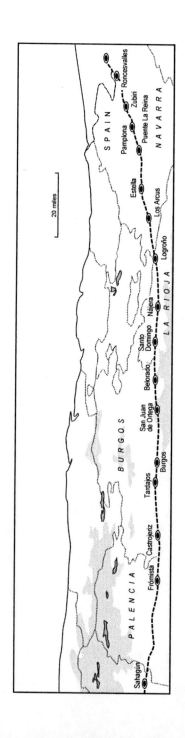

Map of the route to Santiago: From Roncesvalles to Sahagun

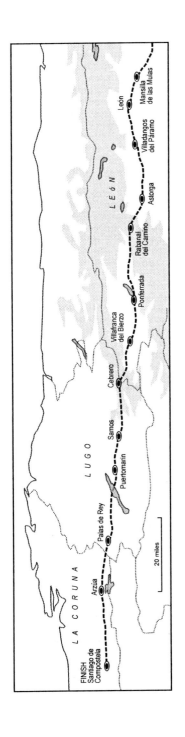

Map of the route to Santiago: From Mansilla de las Mulas to Santiago de Compostela

WALKING FOR WILDLIFE
EL CAMINO TO SANTIAGO DE COMPOSTELA

WALKING FOR WILDLIFE
EL CAMINO TO SANTIAGO DE COMPOSTELA

JEAN ANN BUCK

UPFRONT PUBLISHING
LEICESTERSHIRE

Walking for Wildlife: El Camino to Santiago de Compostela
Copyright © Jean Ann Buck 2004

ISBN 1-84426-283-9

First published 2004 by
UPFRONT PUBLISHING LTD
Leicestershire

Printed by Lightning Source

Foreword

Jean and Ann met in the mid 50s as student teachers at a college on the shores of the Starnbergersee in Bavaria, spending their weekends and time off walking in the mountains. They climbed peaks and walked into Austria. Hitch-hiking, they visited cities, castles, the Black Forest and beyond.

From Germany they travelled by train down to Italy, Ann hauling an old cabin trunk crammed with the works of Shakespeare and her riding gear! They worked for NATO, Jean as a typing instructor, Ann as an accounts clerk. They both married in Italy, attending each other's weddings as bridesmaids and making their own dresses. But all this could be another story!

Their friendship continued over the years and they met up to walk, in the Cotswolds, Cornwall, the Isle of Man and, almost half a century on, the road to Santiago.

Contents

Foreword   *v*

Introduction
 THE ROAD TO SANTIAGO 1

Wednesday 9th May
 JOURNEY TO RONCESVALLES 3

Thursday 10th May
 RONCESVALLES TO ZUBIRI..6

Friday 11th May
 ZUBIRI TO PAMPLONA 10

Saturday 12th May
 PAMPLONA TO PUENTA LA REINA...13

Sunday 13th May
 PUENTA LA REINA TO ESTELLA 18

Monday 14th May
 ESTELLA TO LOS ARCOS 22

Tuesday 15th May
 LOS ARCOS TO VIANA 25

Wednesday 16th May
 VIANA TO LOGRONO AND NAVARETTE 28

Thursday 17th May
 NAVARETTE TO NAJERA...32

Friday 18th May
 NAJERA TO AZOFRA 34

Saturday 19th May
 AZOFRA TO SANTO DOMINGO DE LA CALZADA 38

Sunday 20th May
 SANTO DOMINGO DE LA CALZADA..43

Monday 21st May
SANTO DOMINGO DE LA CALZADA TO SAN JUAN DE ORTEGA 46

Tuesday 22nd May
SAN JUAN DE ORTEGA TO BURGOS.. 51

Wednesday 23rd May
BURGOS TO SAHAGUN 55

Thursday 24th May
SAHAGUN TO CALZADILLA HERMANILLOS....................................... 59

Friday 25th May
CALZADILLA HERMANILLAS TO EL BURGO RANEROS 64

Saturday 26th May
EL BURGO RANEROS TO MANSILLA DE LAS MULAS 69

Sunday 27th May
MANSILLA DE LAS MULAS TO LEON 73

Monday 28th May
LEON 78

Tuesday 29th May
LEON TO HOSPITAL DE ORBIGO 81

Wednesday 30th May
HOSPITAL DE ORBIGO TO ASTORGA 86

Thursday 31st May
ASTORGA TO RABANAL DEL CAMINO 93

Friday 1st June
RABANAL DEL CAMINO TO VILLAFRANCA DEL BIERZO 97

Saturday 2nd June
VILLAFRANCA DEL BIERZO TO SARRIA AND PORTOMARIN 104

Sunday 3rd June
PORTOMARIN TO PALAIS DE REI.. 109

Monday 4th June
PALAIS DE REI TO MELIDE 113

Tuesday 5th June
MELIDE TO ARZUA 116

Wednesday 6th June
ARZUA TO SANTIAGO 119

Thursday 7th June
SANTIAGO.. 122

Friday 8th June
SANTIAGO TO HEATHROW 128

Walk in 2002
BACK TO THE CAMINO 131

Friday 30th August
VILLAFRANCA DEL BIERZO TO SAMOS AND TRIACASTELLA 132

Saturday 31st August
TRIACASTELLA TO ALTO DE POIO 136

Sunday 1st September
ALTO DE POIO TO HERREIRAS 139

Monday 2nd September
HERREIRAS TO VILLAFRANCA DEL BIERZO 142

Tuesday 3rd September
O CEBREIRO 145

Biographies
JEAN 147
ANN 148
BARBARA 149
CAROLYN 149
PENNY 150
GWYNETH 150

Bibliography of Works Cited   151

Introduction
THE ROAD TO SANTIAGO

It was back in AD 813 that the bones of the apostle James
(Santiago in Spanish), cousin of Jesus Christ, had been found
in a tomb on a small hill in a place that became known as
Santiago de Compostela. It seems that the body of the
decapitated apostle had been brought here by boat from the
Holy Land, coming ashore at Padron, where today the best
green peppers are grown. Pilgrims at first came in a trickle,
then, in the twelfth-century when Jerusalem was re-
conquered for Islam, a sacred landscape was required in
Europe itself. In the early thirteenth-century there was intense
activity. The alliance between the kings of Navarra, Castilla
and Aragon cemented an alliance with the Benedictine order
in Cluny, offering huge amounts of gold taken in tribute from
the vanquished moors in return for help in strengthening
Christian resistance to Arab influence. French monks and
craftsmen came over the Pyrenees to help supervise and build
the infrastructure of the pilgrim route, building bridges,
hospitals, hospices and towns. The great cathedrals of Burgos,
Leon and Santiago were built and the towns and villages
became a mixture of Romanesque, Gothic and Arabic styles.
Many of the buildings remain today as refuges and hostels for
pilgrims. Compostela became accessible by several different
routes but in the thirteenth-century the most popular was the
so-called French Road as it offered the best facilities and the
highest degree of safety. It began with four great roads across
France which became one at Puente la Reina in Navarre and
the pilgrims crossed the Pyrenees at Roncesvalles. The eastern
route crossed the mountains over the Somport Pass. It was

1

from Roncesvalles that our journey along El Camino 'The Road' began in the month of May 2001.

Wednesday 9th May
JOURNEY TO RONCESVALLES

I met Ann at Heathrow and we flew together to Madrid. The plane was one and a half hours late, so we circled the airport with rucksacks, sticks and heavy boots. We met two avid hikers who were going to a conference in Madrid. They emphasized the importance of weight when hiking, 'Cut everything in half, even the soap,' they advised.

It was very intimidating to us, as we had not attempted these distances before. I was carrying things like aspirins, liniment, a magnifying glass, my favourite teabags, laxatives, all the stuff an aging person might ever need. I realized I would have to ditch most of it and manage.

We flew from Madrid into the medieval city of Pamplona; filled with adventurous joy, we remembered the Hemingway stories of the bull running. I admit we were two arthritic, overweight grandmas (eight grandchildren between us) but inside we felt young and daring, embarking on the walk of a lifetime.

We took a taxi for the 30 km from Pamplona to Roncesvalles. It was dusk when we arrived. We had expected a border town on the Spanish side of the Pyrenees, the gateway to El Camino. The 'town' consisted of a massive grey edifice, a Gothic French monastery surrounded by woodlands, an ominous, foreboding structure. It reminded me of Colditz. The only sign of comfort came from the row of windows with lacy curtains. Surely the overnight accommodation for pilgrims?

There was a pilgrim restaurant next to the Collegiate Church, an inn and a hostel. As our taxi drew up, a monk marched out to welcome us, unsmiling and solemn. We shook hands, overawed, and followed him through a stone passageway to a cold, damp reception room with a row of long wooden tables. Forms, squarely aligned with the edge of the table, were set in each place. Pens were secured firmly with string. Would anyone steal a pen from a monk? Their Catholic school rigidity was showing; it brought back memories of my early school days at Notre Dame.

We quietly sat down, eyes on our work, and began to complete the forms. 'Specify your reasons for taking this walk: spiritual, religious, personal, or recreational.'

I looked at Ann, who was writing busily. Where was the category for 'Early Alzheimer's, temporary insanity?'

Other pilgrims trudged in and silently filled in their forms. An officious young novice issued orders for those who wished to stay overnight. 'Lights out at 8.00 p.m., no smoking, no talking, rooms must be vacated by 7.00 a.m.'

Mass was about to commence. She glared at the backpacking sinners and we knew we ought to attend. But we hadn't walked a kilometre yet, and were feeling regretful already. We waited for our forms to be scrutinized. Ann was first, her pilgrim passport issued and stamped with great flourish, her *direccion* from Florida, USA easily recognized. When it came to my turn, the Isle of Man was unfamiliar. Were we not all from the world of Man?

We unanimously declined to stay and scurried down to the Posada, praying they had a room. We met a New Zealand woman coming back from Mass who was staying in the monastery. She thought there were about eighty people crammed in the dormitories and it was freezing cold.

We were elated to find the hostel had room. Very basic, but comfortable; beautiful, old, red tiled floors, worn unevenly from countless pilgrim feet. We opened the heavy wooden shutters. In the soft evening light we could see the beech trees and the winding pilgrim path. The snow on the Pyrenees glowed in the dusk.

Leaving our rucksacks, we headed back to the monastery and the little pilgrim restaurant, which was warm and welcoming, filled with chattering folk of all nationalities. The same pilgrim menu served all: soup, wine, crusty bread and delicious fresh trout with a creamy ice cream for dessert. All for 1000 *pesetas* – about £4.

We talked to the New Zealanders, who had walked from the French border in 2 ft of snow. It took two days to cover the 23 km. We were so glad we hadn't attempted that section.

Our overnight stay at La Posado cost us about £12 each, worth every penny. We felt so much better after our meal and a hot shower. We set the alarm for 5.30 a.m. and repacked our rucksacks.

Thursday 10th May
RONCESVALLES TO ZUBIRI

Ann's alarm went off. I didn't move! On the hour all night I was awakened to the bleep of that watch. I was tired and irritable. Ann promised to keep it under her pillow tonight. We finally started on our way at 7.00 a.m. The monastery was still shuttered. There was a mist on the hills and a chill in the air.

We began the Camino, which was well marked with yellow arrows or a scallop shell sign – the emblem of the pilgrimage from medieval times. Passed a fourteenth-century Gothic pilgrim cross, along a gravel path flanked by beech trees, well manicured and surprisingly park-like for the first few kilometres. We continually adjusted our rucksacks.

Several well-muscled walkers passed us by at cracking speed. '*Bon Camino*,' they called as they forged ahead.

The easy wooded path petered out at the little village of Burguete, where, according to legend, Roland, Oliveros and King Marsilius perished alongside 40,000 Christian and Saracen troops. A French priest, Aymeric Picaud from Poitou travelled the Camino in the 1100s. He wrote in 1130 a guidebook in Latin with a wealth of detail. It is one of the most delightful and revealing documents on the Pilgrim Way. Here is his report on the Battle at Burguete:

> Charlemagne was crossing the path with Ganelon Turpin and 20,000 Christians with Roland and Oliveros and 20,000 soldiers bringing up the rearguard when Marsillius and Beligando (the Moorish caliphs) and 50,000 Saracens came out at dawn from the forests and hills where, at Ganelon's treacherous counsel, they had hidden themselves for two days

and two nights and divided their army into two corps, one of 20,000 men and the other of 30,000. The 20,000 ambushed our rearguard; but our men turned at once against them and after fighting from dawn until the hour of Terce (nine o'clock in the morning) forced them to succumb, each and every one of them; not one of the 20,000 escaped with his life. But at once the other 30,000 Saracens attacked our men, who were weak and exhausted after such a mighty combat, and slew them all, big and small. (Lozano, 1999)

Here at Burguete where the route divided, we had to decide which path to take. Frogs jumped and splashed at our feet, as we stood in the marsh that was freely intermingled with cowpats.

Four German walkers loomed through the mist. 'This way a little longer, but much better,' they bellowed. Their marching feet echoed across the bridge and they rapidly disappeared into the distance.

We hauled on our rucksacks and followed their muddy footprints across the bridge. Old farm buildings, tinkling of cowbells, the smell of hay and chicks and chickens everywhere as we headed for the village of Espinal. Charming well kept houses with brightly painted shutters, flowerpots and window boxes festooned with geraniums and petunias welcomed us. We walked the pavement, flanked by open drains.

It was 9.00 a.m. and, at last, what joy – a café, filled with pilgrims, rucksacks everywhere and walking sticks dangled from chairs. I rushed to the bar, crossed my legs and ordered *café con leche* (coffee with milk) and *tostado* with *marmelada* and headed straight for the loo!

The group of New Zealanders we had met last night were about to leave as we arrived. The café was warm and comfortable, full of excited, chattering pilgrims.

We walked through hamlets of plastered, painted medieval buildings: Mezquiriz, Viscarret, Linzoain; farming communities with well tended stock and horses grazing in the fields. By the path a mare protected her newborn foal. We struggled up the slate track over steep hills; mud and clay

7

clotted our boots. It took hours to reach Zubiri. We descended through pines, beeches and oaks and came upon great stone slabs known as Roland's Footsteps, a reminder of the great French hero. As we came into Zubiri there was an ancient building now in ruins. Centuries ago it was the inn on the pass, the first refuge for the pilgrims from Roncesvalles.

Despite the mud and overcast sky, it was a wonderful journey today, with plenty of birdsong; banks of golden cowslips, which I hadn't seen since my childhood days in Suffolk; violets, wild columbine, orchids (twayblade, a creamy orchid with ochre specks), oregano, marjoram, lots of gorse (reminding me of the Isle of Man), vetch and a beautiful blue flower I didn't know.

We left the Camino track and crossed the Gothic bridge into Zubiri (which is Basque for the 'village of the bridge'). It had two semicircular arches, which crossed the River Arga. It was known as the Bridge of Rabies, after a traditional local ritual of driving livestock three times around its central pillar to rid them of the disease.

We walked to the municipal hostel to find the New Zealand party already there, washing their boots and hanging out clothes to dry. We had a look at the cramped musty dorms – the one dirty loo and the shower full of scum and decided, 'No! We'll find somewhere else.'

A bare-footed German backpacker sat on the pavement outside the hostel, staring bemusedly at the small hiking boots he held in his hand. 'I do not understand, my shoes have gone,' he said 'where is the thief and why?'

We walked to a café and met the New Zealanders again. The boot mystery was solved; they chortled over the fact they had mistaken the German's muddy boots for their own and scrubbed them clean, but now they couldn't find him anywhere. These were tough sinewy farmers' wives, who had scant sympathy for slackers. They explained the presence of so many New Zealanders on the trail. A book had been written about the Camino two years ago by one of their countrymen. Now many Kiwis had taken up the walk.

After the meal we asked for the nearest hotel. The owner showed us a smart block of rooms at the rear of the restaurant. We shopped at a store for water and picnic items for tomorrow, increasing the weight of the rucksacks by pounds!

In the quiet hotel room, we threw off our muddy boots and crashed onto the beds exhausted. We had covered 23 km. After a nap, I ran a huge bath and wallowed like a hippo! Somebody had left behind a foot restoring lotion; I rubbed it on in hope. We slept very well!

Friday 11th May
ZUBIRI TO PAMPLONA

Left at dawn – back over the Bridge of Rabies on a rough uphill track that made for slow going to Osteriz. The New Zealanders marched by; we were agog. Their shoulders padded with fleece, tubes swung from rucksacks to provide instant drinking water. Leather and Gortex boots gleamed magnificently in the dawn. They showed no pain as they strode on. Ann floundered, her sleeping bag wrapped in a Sainsbury's carrier bag looked the worse for wear. Tied to the top of her rucksack it wobbled and tilted at every step.

Halfway up the track we stopped on a bend for a breather and a pee. Ann hid behind a bush and changed her clothes, hurling items willy-nilly into the shrub along with her pee-soaked trousers. Freshly clad in shorts, shivering in the breeze, sleeping bag now buried in her lightened pack, she struggled on uphill. As we screamed with laughter, more pilgrims began climbing the hill. One carried a tripod and camera gear. This was Richard, an American, photographing the pilgrim route for a book; trailed by his Texan colleague, Russ. A slim Indian lady walked by; her head and shoulders wrapped in a sari, she looked comfortable and cool. Toting a small backpack, she picked herbs from the grassy bank and stepped lightly and elegantly along.

From Osteriz the track wound around enormous gravel pits and a medieval hamlet with mellow stone farmhouses. It took a long time to get to Larrasoana; we followed the path onto the main road and crossed the Arga river again. Once over the bridge, hungry for breakfast, we looked for a bar, wandered through the village and came to a little café by the river. Seated at the tables, lolling in the morning sunshine were the New Zealanders. Backpacks were stacked against the wall and unsaintly pilgrims elbowed each other to grab coffee from the counter. The cheerful proprietor was on to a winner as his was the only café for miles. We unpacked our breakfast (yogurt, bananas and juice), purchased coffee and a croissant the size of a bus and settled down to eat like hogs in the warm sun. The New Zealand team gave us some water donated by a passing camper van. We were dubious about Spanish water and drank bottled whenever we could.

Towards Pamplona, the track was almost impassable: rough, rocky and deep in mud. But flowers bloomed in immoderate profusion. There were banks of wild crocus, columbines and hedge upon hedge of dog roses and the smell of May everywhere.

We stopped for lunch where the route divided and enjoyed cream cheese, apples and chocolate. On our way, the lower route led to Arleta along the old Roman road before descending to Pamplona. There were groves of trees and lush grass, horse bells clanked on the hillside and sheep clustered around stone water troughs. Houses of crumbling stone with bars and shutters on all the windows were covered with climbing roses. The gnarled trunks supported blooms the size of cabbages. Bees hummed around like a gathering of Zeppelins.

We were tired and hot when we finally arrived in the suburbs of Burlada on the outskirts of Pamplona. 'Look out for the Renault dealer on Calle Mayor,' the guide read. The garage was no longer there but the Renault sign remained. Over the Magdalena Bridge, joy: Pamplona! Wrong! Another 4 km through Pamplona suburbia, yellow arrows and shell symbols cleverly hidden in obscure places. Near exhaustion, we climbed up into the old city surrounded by the massive sixteenth-century walls with the cathedral rising above. Grey-faced and weary, we stumbled through the park and climbed several hundred steps.

Ann faltered in a doorway and asked the Spanish lady peering through the archway, '*Donde una hostel, hotel*?'

The senora pointed to the next doorway and beckoned us to follow her. We trooped behind; we didn't care where she led, white slaver, terrorist or whatever.

Oh Lord, four more flights of stairs to climb. It was an ancient, dilapidated building with huge beams and ornate chipped tiling. We were shown into a large room with four beds and a little balcony overlooking the old city rooftops.

We lay unmoving on the beds and shared the remains of our biscuits and apples, too exhausted to descend four flights to look for dinner. I tried to write in my journal; my shaky, spidery handwriting resembled my grandmother's. I fell asleep with my pen in my hand.

Saturday 12th May
PAMPLONA TO PUENTA LA REINA

We rose early and fumbled our way around the rambling old building, the wide cracked floorboards squeaked at every move. The bedroom door was double-paned glass and curtained; it didn't shut properly and opened noisily. No one was up when we left at dawn; it required two of us to unlatch the door. We lifted the heavy wooden bar, swung it to one side and stepped out into the old town.

We decided to bus out of town. The thought of traversing miles of suburbs was depressing. I longed for a hot drink, but the city was still sleeping, the sky was turning pale with the dawn.

Hurray, there were buses in the square! We jumped on the Cizur Mayor line, which ended 4 km beyond Pamplona. A quiet suburb, row upon row of new houses; nothing to indicate we were near the Camino. The bus driver shook his head and kept repeating 'Cizur Mayor, no Cizur Menor.' Major not Minor! We looked at the route map and realized our mistake. Cizur Menor! I decided there must be a short cut across town rather than return to Pamplona. It had been a long, gradual climb out of the city and I didn't fancy walking back. The town was still asleep. The streets were empty, no one to give us directions. As we passed a house we saw a girl opening her bedroom window. Waving frantically to gain her attention, we explained the confusion with town names and the missing Camino. Her father, who spoke English and was still clad in pyjamas, leaned unsteadily out of his bedroom window to give us complicated directions. We smiled and waved to show we had understood and walked on, hoping

Dad didn't crash onto his front lawn in his valiant efforts to help. At a junction with roads curling off in all directions there was a sign that showed Menor 3.5 km ahead. We crossed the road as a little Seat drew up: pyjama-clad dad offered to taxi us to Menor! He sweetly ignored our mud-crusted boots and drove us to the monastery gate.

Menor refuge was quiet and peaceful; the pilgrims had left hours earlier. Opposite the refuge was a bar and restaurant. I suggested to Ann that we stop for coffee and breakfast, but she wanted to keep moving.

'There will be plenty of stops en route. We are already behind schedule,' she insisted.

I plodded on, feeling cross, thirsty and hungry. I moaned continually for the next few kilometres, nibbled on raisins and sipped water. The track led through lush farmland.

We met a young Spaniard who walked with us to the next village, proudly practising his English, which he had learned in Spanish Miami. We were in the 'bowl of Pamplona' he told us.

We followed a stream and walked through the ruined village of Guendulain and started a 2 km climb out of the 'bowl' into the foothills of the Sierra. Reeling with exhaustion through Zariquiegui, we came to a fountain of fresh cold drinking water. This is the Fuenta de Reniega – The Fountain of Denial. We joined the queue of Pilgrims waiting to fill their bottles. According to legend, an exhausted and parched traveller was tempted by the devil, who offered to show him this spring to quench his thirst in return for denying his faith. The pilgrim resisted and was rewarded by the appearance of an apostle garbed in pilgrim clothing who gave him water from a scallop shell. The devil would have found us easy prey as we were down to our last few sips.

There was no café, or shop here; just the little church with a blaze of pansies in chipped earthenware pots outside. We sat in the sun and dug in our rucksacks to find the cheese we had saved and some raisins and pumpkin seeds. Never had such a small snack tasted so good and felt so filling. The cold water was delicious.

Among the many pilgrims on the slopes were Bente and Josef, a Dutch couple who were making the walk for the second time. Both Bente and Josef are cancer survivors and had undergone surgery; Bente, for a mastectomy, and Josef, for prostrate cancer. They planned to take three or four months to complete the walk, but Josef found it hard going.

In their younger days when they had done their first Camino they said it was one of the happiest times of their lives. They were trying to recapture some of this joy.

We faced another long haul up to the highest point of the Sierra du Perdon; the site of theological disputes and battles – the hills of Perdon or forgiveness! A test for all our strengths. My rucksack top strap had come apart and Josef insisted he would stitch it for me, but I knotted it with string and plodded on. Richard, the photographer, charged by and complained his photographic gear weighed him down.

The New Zealanders were picnicking en route and waved. A young family of New Zealanders, mother, father and two young daughters, one with a teddy bear mascot strapped to her back, greeted us and marched on.

A young American boy from Los Angeles who had arrived that morning at Pamplona airport joined the Camino. Ill-clad without a pack, little money and flimsy sandals, he aimed to complete the walk to Santiago and back by July for the feast of San Fermin – the running of the bulls through Pamplona. I questioned his footwear. He would walk barefoot part of the way if necessary, he replied. I wondered how long he would last.

On the Sierra del Perdon, there is a long copper-coloured sculpture depicting a procession of medieval pilgrims carrying flags, riding donkeys and horses leaning forward into the wind.

It was breezy on top of Perdon. A line of white windmills stretched over the ridge. The views were splendid – the whole

Pamplona basin lay before us with a backdrop of the Pyrenees. We followed a gorse track to the steep rocky descent into Uterga. There were banks of marjoram and thyme. The air was filled with the smell of herbs.

Ann slowed going downhill, but goodness knows why – I managed to get a cracking pace with rocks and stones tumbling around my feet. I found uphill the worst and Ann pulled ahead of me then, as I huffed and puffed along. Ann's trek stick had given her hand blisters so she wore a woolly red glove for protection!

My stick, light and tough, came from Switzerland and was a present from me to my father forty-six years ago. It has all the plaques on it from the places I visited in Switzerland. I felt close to my father as I trudged along. My stick was a great conversation point and much admired.

We walked with Bente and Josef on a long asphalt track into the village of Muruzabel. We were tired and hungry. It was siesta time and everywhere was quiet. We found a small bar and fell with joy into the door, only to find the owner was closing. He suggested we go to his house and he would prepare refreshments. We followed his directions but were unable to find the place. In despair, we knocked on a door that seemed the likely one, but the senora who answered irritably reminded us that it was siesta.

I apologised and asked where I could get food and drink. The senor came to the door and ordered his wife and daughter to prepare a meal. She reluctantly waved us inside and her daughter, aged about seventeen, began to lay the table and invited us to sit down.

The chairs were dilapidated. The broken springs in my chair viciously jabbed my bottom every time I moved.

We were served orange squash, salad, tepid cups of instant soup and freshly made omelettes. Ravenously, we bolted the food down as fast as it was placed on the table. *Postre* (dessert) was lemon flan, which was delicious.

Truly grateful, we offered payment. Senora entered the scene and demanded 2,000 pesetas each, a preposterous amount. We looked sheepishly at each other, paid and left. Josef said we were paying for the girl to go through college! We wondered if they were going to buy new chairs, or were they Basques saving up to join the 'separatist' movement!

It was a tough walk today: 21 km by the time we reached Puenta la Reina. The Roncesvalles and Somport routes converged at the entrance. Bente, Josef, Ann and I walked on the main road and met pilgrims coming into town from all directions. At the junction of the two routes there is a memorial statue to the pilgrimage. To celebrate the 1965 Holy Year, Gerardo Brun was commissioned to cast a statue of Santiago Peregrino.

There was a smart three-star hotel ahead, with a pilgrim sign outside. I walked into reception, where my mud-covered boots and splattered trousers made me look like a bag lady.

The receptionist pointed to the basement. Beds for pilgrims downstairs, for 1,000 pesetas a night. Bente and Josef had walked on to the refuge, where they took the last bunks. However, downstairs we had a choice of bunks and clean showers and toilets. Bliss. We did our washing in the well-equipped laundry room.

Other pilgrims arrived: Germans, Austrians and Spaniards. There was a lot of pilgrim spirit; exchange of stories, tired laughter and maps unrolled for the next day. Everyone was asleep and snoring by 8.30 p.m.

Sunday 13th May
PUENTE LA REINA TO ESTELLA

The Puente la Reina hotel served a breakfast buffet but the dining room didn't open until 7.00 a.m. We decided on a late start; after all it was Sunday and maybe we wouldn't be able to find anything open en route. The buffet was a sight for sore eyes: crusty rolls, butter, cheese and ham, croissants, cereal, juice and fruit! Wow – we were first in the door! We made up doggy bags for our backpacks and followed the yellow arrows out of town.

Puente le Reina (The Queen's Bridge) – was named in honour of its sponsor, Dona Mayor, wife of Sancho III (1000–1035), who had the bridge built to accommodate the influx of pilgrims. It is one of the most famous bridges on our route, with six arches and five pillars, in an elegantly curved design.

We followed the main Calle Mayor through town and stopped at an old sugar factory to watch the storks nesting on top of the factory tower. We arrived at the little village of Eunea where an enterprising shopkeeper had opened for the pilgrim trade. Despite all our goodies we decided to buy some bread and cheese for tomorrow. We had still not accepted the limitations of our backpacks and our ability to carry much weight.

We continued on a track that became narrow, winding and very rugged. At Maneru we followed the path through orchards and vegetable plots and crossed a bridge into the wonderful, enchanting medieval village of Cirauqui; cyclamen, geraniums and petunias cascaded from the balconies. Cirauqui is Basque for 'vipers nest' because of the rocky hill it was built upon, and the bandits who lived there.

We wound round the thirteenth-century church of San Roman on the rocky hillside. A horse and new foal grazed on the bank below.

> At the exit from Ciraqui, a recently restored stretch of Roman paving leads down the hill to a Roman bridge. Although almost the entire pilgrimage road follows the Roman Via Traiana, these are by far the most spectacular remains. You will follow Roman paving, with some stretches repaired or rebuilt in the Middle Ages, most of the way from here to Lorca (Gitlitz and Davidson, 2000:91–92).

We joined Bente and Josef picnicking on the other side of the bridge; they had abandoned their socks and boots and were sunning themselves. We followed suit, delved into our doggy bags and ate a hearty picnic accompanied by the sound of the frogs on the riverbank. It took torture and talcum powder to resume our boots. We vowed never to take them off en route again.

This was one of the most beautiful days. There were banks of poppies, hedgerows of dog roses and honeysuckle and birdsong everywhere. We saw a field full of greenfinches swooping and diving after insects. We descended into the Yerra Valley and passed a ruined medieval village – their foundations covered with dog roses and vines. We crossed the Salado River by a double arched bridge.

Aymeric Picaud wrote in his Pilgrim guide of 1130:

> Take care not to drink the water here, neither yourself nor your horse, for it is a deadly river. On the way to Santiago we came across two Navarrese sitting by the bank, sharpening the knives they used to flay pilgrims' horses which had drunk the water and died. We asked them if the water was fit to drink, and they lyingly replied that it was, whereupon we gave it to our horses to drink. Two of them dropped dead at once and the Navarrese flayed them there and then. (Lozano, 1999)

On to Lorca, where I filled my bottle at the grand drinking fountain. Our map told us to cross the N111 main road by way of an underpass. We found the underpass overgrown and derelict. Cars sped along the main road above us, so we were taking our lives in our hands as we dashed across.

It was a tiring 7 km into Estella. The last kilometres of the day were the worst. The hostel was crowded with pilgrims of all nationalities queuing for admittance.

The bunk beds were jammed together; there were only four top bunks left. I didn't want a top bed, as I knew it would be a drama to get down in the night for the loo! A Brazilian gave up his bottom bunk to Ann and a very dignified middle-aged Englishman offered me his lower bunk. We were impressed with their kindness, and didn't know until the next day that it was traditional for the young to give up their lower bunks for the elderly!

The well-organized Englishman above me left to boil eggs for lunch the next day. I was impressed. Why hadn't I thought of boiling eggs? The kitchen was sparsely furnished with one or two pots and pans and a few chipped mugs. The Indian lady was in the kitchen, her hair freshly washed and plaited. She was drinking a brew from all the herbs she had collected.

Getting ready for bed was a three-act play. The shower room was opposite my bunk and pilgrims streamed in and out. The loo was at the other end of the dormitory.

I had made a long nightdress from silk cut off the bolt I used for silk painting. It was a yard wide and two yards long, folded and stitched up the side with a gap at the top for my arms and a hole at the top for my head; all very crude, but warm and lightweight. Stuffing clothes into my rucksack and scrabbling into my sleeping bag in this voluminous nightdress was not easy.

Lights out was at 9.00 p.m. I struggled blindly with the zip on my sleeping bag; I couldn't get it together.

Tossing and turning and rocking the bed in desperation to zip myself up, my top bunkmate looked over the side and whispered down, 'Is something wrong?'

I told him, 'I can't zip myself in.'

'Hang on,' he said, 'I'll see what I can do,' and climbed down in his skimpy shorts, his bits and pieces in full view. He tucked my flowing silk into the bag and zipped me inside!

I lay there wondering how I was going to go to the loo, while Ann wept tears of hysterical laughter into her pillow. Sleep came anyway, regardless of all the snoring around me.

In the early hours, I quietly unzipped my bag, made sure it didn't fall on the floor, and crept down to the loo in my silk nightshirt, looking like a ghost in the shadows.

Monday 14th May
ESTELLA TO LOS ARCOS

We had booked and paid for breakfast at the hostel. By the time we had finished in the bathroom and packed our rucksacks, we were last down to the kitchen. No hot milk and no bread, but Bente and Joseph were waiting, eager to tell us about the ghost a pilgrim had seen in the night! They decided this was to be a rest day for them. They planned to walk to Irache, take the main road for a while and then bus to Los Arcos.

Having done this route before, they were aware of the tedious areas and today's route covered a 12 km stretch without villages. The asphalt path followed the N111 through endless cornfields and vineyards. The bus idea sounded attractive and we agreed to spend the day with them.

Estella was an important town on the pilgrim route. In 1090, a new district was created for French settlers on the left bank of the River Ega. Trade flourished and the left bank became a privileged position. The Jewish settlement were forced to move and build their homes on the side of castle hill; the former synagogue became a church in 1145, dedicated to Santa Maria Jus de Castillo.

Over the centuries, new districts were created, each having their own church and hospital. On the orders of Charles V in 1524, they merged and a new hospital was built for contagious patients, outside the town. Until the founding of the hospice at Estella, pilgrims were attended by the Monastery of Santa Maria la Real de Irache, on the outskirts. We planned to take that route and avail ourselves of the *Bodega's* free wine fountain.

We took our time leaving Estella. Josef wanted to show us the stone carvings of Roland and Charlemagne, the only civic building on the route to portray them. This was an amazing town with priceless monuments; artists had flocked here during the centuries of its prosperity.

It was a lovely day, warm and sunny. We walked along the main road towards Logrono. Shouts of '*Bon Camino*' came from the cars as they whizzed along, blasting their horns in greeting. We climbed gently into Irache, on the north slope of Montejurra.

Pilgrims were already lined up at the wine fountain, waiting for it to start flowing at 10.00 a.m. A German motorcyclist roared up, and a team of French cyclists – everyone clutched plastic bottles! The *Bodega* is a grand building with an ornate fountain with two spigots constructed on the courtyard wall, one of fresh water and one of red wine. A bas-relief of a pilgrim observed the thirsty pilgrims below.

I took a drink of this 'wholesome and restorative local Navarrese wine' (to quote the guide) and filled a small bottle. Josef and Bente hauled out two large bottles – good luck to them!

The vast monastery sprawling across the hillside had records of its Benedictine community dating back to 958.

We followed the path to Azqueta and walked through a suburb onto the main N111. We crossed the road to a hotel and café near the bus stop, and relaxed in the comfy chairs drinking *café con leche* until the bus arrived. This was hardly a day of pilgrim toil! We were in jolly spirits from the wine fountain.

We reached the hostel at Los Arcos before opening time. It was a fairly new building on a side street in the town centre. A former teachers' dwelling behind a school, it was now the municipal hostel.

We sat on the porch as a trickle of pilgrims arrived.

Our passports were stamped and we had a choice of beds. I washed laundry and left it to dry in the afternoon sun. We enjoyed a really nice late lunch (or early dinner) in the town. Back to the hostel for a nap (red wine)! I wrote cards to grandchildren. They stretch from Los Angeles to Brussels.

The place filled. Richard and his mate, Russ from Texas, joined us in our dorm. The Indian lady checked in the bed by the window. Fascinated, I watched her every move. One sari was washed, the other draped over the head of her bed. She had such a small rucksack that I wondered if she wore everything! How did she manage to remain immaculate?

Everyone was amazed we made it to Los Arcos in such good time. We shamefacedly admitted that we bussed 12 km. I was ribbed for the rest of the evening about all those lost miles for wildlife. How could I do such a thing, when the birds and flowers depended on me?

The medieval town of Los Arcos was built on the site of a Roman town. The most notable building is the church, dating back to the twelfth-century. The town belonged to the crown of Castile from 1463 to 1753 and became a thriving centre for foreign exchange and toll collection. It once had a leprosarium at Ermita de San Blas. Leprous pilgrims were not allowed into the town, but nevertheless made the pilgrimage in the hope of cure as Christ had cured Lazarus.

I had six teabags in my rucksack, carefully hoarded since the Isle of Man. Tonight I made two cups of English tea. Nectar! The hostels had very little crockery. Mugs and cups were cracked and chipped. We decided to buy tin mugs and hang them from our packs and clank along like other pilgrims.

The second problem was toilet paper! Thieving pilgrims stole reams of it to take on the road! The *refugios* were loo-roll-less by the time we arrived. Purchases en route were difficult. We never arrived anywhere until siesta, when the shops were closed.

Despite our less strenuous day, we were in bed and asleep by 9.00 p.m.!

In the bowl of Pamplona

Ann plus sleeping bag, en route Pamplona

Top: The Sierre del Perdon sculpture
Bottom: Sorting the rucksack, Pamplona

Top: Ann plus poppies, en route Puenta La Reina
Bottom: Footpaths through fields, Maneru

A slurp at the wine fountain, Irache

Resting with the climbing roses, Azofra

The Muslim boundary stone, Alesanco

The derelict village of Espinosa

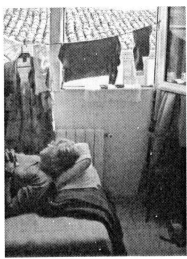

Top: The horseshoe arch, Villafranca Montes de Oca
Bottom: Snoozing with the laundry, Sahagun

Top: With the German pilgrims, Sahagun
Bottom: The Franciscan and Benedictine mural, Sahagun

Ann, a dot on the horizon, en route Calzadilla Hermanillos

Top: Pilgrim statue, Mansilla de las Mulas
Bottom: Stork nests on every tower, en route Leon

The courtyard statues, Hostel san Marcos, Leon

The bronze statue, Leon

One boot, one sandal, Leon

Top: Dreary trudge out of Mansilla
Bottom: Foot care from the vet, Mansilla

Foot 'airing' at dawn, en route Leon

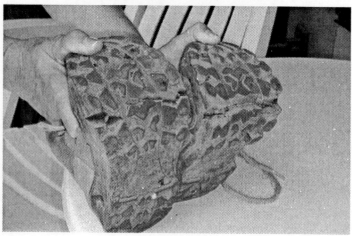

Top: Pavement respite, Leon
Bottom: The worn boots, Leon

Tuesday 15th May
LOS ARCOS TO VIANA

We rose early and were on the road by 7.00 a.m. A distance of 19 km to Viana today. A narrow lane took us past the cemetery, originally the site of the old hospital for contagious diseases. The gate was inscribed with a warning: *'Yo que fui lo que tú eres, tú serás lo que yo soy.'* ('I was once what you are, and you will be what I am!')

> Between Los Arcos and the first hospital you come to, there flows a river which is deadly poisonous to all horses and men who drink from it. Every river between Estella and Logrono is unhealthy for man and beast alike and the fish are poisonous. (Aymeric Picaud, circa 1130) (Lozano, 1999)

The lane became a dirt track, running parallel to the N111. The path was occasionally obscured by cropland, but we followed the yellow arrows and saw the village of Sansol in the distance. Poppies flanked the wheat fields and there was a view of the distant mountains.

Ann tucked four poppies into her hatband, one for each grandchild. 'I'll do this every day,' she said. 'Carry my treasures with me all the way to Santiago.'

As we climbed higher there were banks of cistus and rosemary.

We could hear the church clocks chiming and the bells ringing as we neared Sansol. Over the N111, down the steep path to the Linares river. Then a short climb to Torres del Rio, which was located in the valley. This village still had remnants of its city wall; it was the location of one of the architectural jewels of the Camino. The church featured a semicircular apse, a round tower, and a lantern crowning the dome on the roof. Lanterns like this acted as beacons to guide the pilgrims to their destination.

As we passed under the arch into the square we saw the Indian lady again. She sat on a bench, a little apart from the motley group of pilgrims, who cheerfully breakfasted outside in a courtyard.

As we purchased apples and bananas in a nearby shop, a procession of familiar rucksacks wobbled past: Sybole, a German girl, Richard and Russ, Bente and Josef. Here was an excuse to linger in the sunshine and enjoy a cup of coffee with our friends.

Onward to Viana: 10 km and no villages. On the hillside overlooking the snow-capped mountains surrounded by flowers and herbs, sheltered by almond trees, we ate our picnic lunch.

It was a hot afternoon. The path descended a ravine called the *Barranco Mataburros* (Mulekiller Ravine). We slipped and slithered in the sand and gravel; it was a tough road for pilgrims and their heavy backpacks, as well as for mules. Through vineyards, almond and olive groves until we reached a river, the Cornava. There was an old Roman settlement, abandoned and derelict.

It was a stiff climb into Viana to the refuge, a restored building next to the church. It was full; Bente and Josef had already arrived and saved us the last two bunks, but here they were three-tiered and the top two were left.

I took a look at the cramped room and the height of the bunks and decided against it. We accepted the warden's offer to telephone and arrange a room in a private house. The owner had agreed to take the pilgrim overflow.

Viana's imposing walls were an indication of its past status as a heavily fortified frontier town. Viana is full of majestic old mansions, some four storeys high, each bearing a family crest, and it was in one of these houses that we stayed.

It was an imposing house with the original tiled floors and staircase, carved doors and blackened beams, full of ancestral paintings, tapestries and dark, heavy furniture. We had an airy room with a fireplace, sitting area and a little balcony overlooking the rooftops to the hills we had just travelled. The old doorway led into the grand hallway opposite, which was the family chapel, complete with pews and embroidered, tasselled kneeling cushions. In the corner of our room was an old portrait of a man in uniform emblazoned with medals. Perhaps he was an important Spanish aristocrat?

I washed my clothes and hung them surreptitiously outside on the balcony, reluctant to damage the ambience of this palace. We descended the staircase to the bathroom with polished brass taps, marble basins and a footed bathtub deep enough to marinate an elephant. I felt like a clod-footed peasant, afraid of contaminating the place!

We were tired and very hungry. The bars and restaurants were open so we decided to venture out for a meal. We carried the huge door key with us. It was a heavy iron object, big enough to unlock Buckingham Palace or brain three Grenadier guards! The restaurants were busy but we decided on a small cosy one a few minutes from the house. We propped the key against the table leg and had a delicious meal of fish, salad and a bottle of red wine. Sitting in a snug corner seat with the soft candlelight and warm surroundings, I started to nod off with a forkful of salad in my hand!

Back at the house, we climbed into goose feather beds with white broderie anglais bed covers and slept like logs!

Wednesday 16th
VIANA TO LOGRONO AND NAVARETTE

The archaic town mansion was an expensive museum – 3,500 pesetas each. Resentfully, we paid. The refuge had told us we would be charged 1,500, but the capricious owner had misled them and scalped anyone she felt had money. She emphasized her habit of praying in the family chapel every day. For manna from the pilgrims? We left at dawn, a little tetchy.

It was too early for a café bar, but I was determined to get coffee and breakfast before we began the Camino. As we wound down the steep hill out of town, I saw a large building with a flashing neon sign. It was a biscuit factory. Opposite was a café bar full of workers and van drivers enjoying their breakfast.

The air was thick with smoke and the floor covered with food wrappers and cigarette butts. The coffee and baking smelled wonderful; a change from the arid mausoleum of the previous night. We were a source of interest to the lively crowd, who cheered and wished us *Bon Camino* as we walked away.

On to the main road and back to the Camino path. The track took us through vineyards and olive groves to the hermitage La Trinidad de Cuevas. We crossed the boundary between Navarre and La Rioja. This was an extensive wetland area and nature reserve called Pantano de las Canas (*pantano* translates as wetlands/swamp), a protected area and bird sanctuary. The bird life was disappointing.

We skirted the hill, site of the ancient city of Cantabria. There were ongoing excavations revealing new data on the pre-Roman settlement, but these were concealed from public view. We had hoped to see much more on our way to Logrono.

The asphalt track climbed gradually all the way to town. There was a ghetto area on the outskirts. Piles of stinking garbage, mangy barking dogs who leapt at their fences as we walked by, people living in shacks with grubby partially-clothed children, stacks of wood and rusted cars.

In contrast, the pilgrim route entered the city via the great Puente de Piedra (Bridge of Stone), built at the end of the nineteenth-century to replace the medieval bridge over the Ebro river. The view of the cathedral from the bridge was a breathtaking sight. Work was being carried out on the bridge pilgrim path. A scallop shell pattern was being set in stone. We trod carefully between the workmen.

We met Sybole, Bente and Josef outside a café in the main square. They suggested we leave our rucksacks with the café owner who would keep an eye on them while we toured the city.

It was heavenly to be packless. Shopping! At a dusty hardware store we rummaged through the shelves for tin mugs. Ann found an army water bottle. With her khaki shorts, knobbly knees and camouflage water bottle, she looked like an aging Girl Guide. I treated myself to a pair of shorts and a nightgown. The time had come to abandon the silk nightdress and lay the ghostly legend to rest!

Our final chore was the bank cash machine. We found a shop selling sweets, dried fruits and nuts and stocked up.

We moved on to visit the thirteenth-century church of San Bartolome.

The interior has been recently and spectacularly restored, so that you will see the stone elements of construction in all their functional purity (even as you will realize that in their original state they would have been covered with brightly painted biblical scenes). The apse is Romanesque in the Jaca style. The arches over the crossing are the earliest Gothic, with heavy, slightly pointed forming arches holding up the weight of the vaults. The capitals are still Romanesque in their size and motif. (Gitlitz and Davidson, 2000: 128).

The route to Navarette and Najera sounded grim; I quote: 'Make your way through an industrial estate. Next you have to cross a ring road and go through an area of rubbish dumps...' Enough, bus time again!

We gathered our packs and walked to the *estacion* on the other side of town and bussed the 10 km to Navarrete. Up the hill to the hostel which, as usual, was adjacent to the church.

It was a newly restored building, clean and fresh with immaculate bed linen. The wardens at the hostel were volunteers; 'salt of the earth' ladies, practical and hospitable, who welcomed us as friends. We were invited to the communal dinner, which was given every evening. This is financed by the contributions of the previous day's pilgrims. Therefore dinner can be sparse or splendid.

I had been feeling under the weather all day. I had a sore throat and decided to find a pharmacy. I bought paracetamol and soothing throat tablets, took a hot shower, then put on a brave face for the evening ahead. We went to matins in the sixteenth-century church, triple-aisled, with a magnificent gilded and painted *retablo* (the framed area behind the altar).

After the service, the priest proudly invited the pilgrims to an ante-room filled with church treasures in glass-fronted cabinets. There were decorated manuscripts, gold and silver chalices encrusted with jewels and statues from Peru hundreds of years old.

A mouse ran out from under a cupboard! Someone said this happened every night! How strange; maybe it's clockwork! Poor church mouse didn't apply here, this was a treasure trove. I thought of the slums we had passed on the way; couldn't some of this stuff be used to help these people?

It was a lovely evening at the hostel. The table was laid with candles and bottles of wine. There was salad, soup and a chickpea casserole with vegetables, followed by fruit and more wine to wash it down. Many nationalities were at the table –

French, Germans, an Australian girl, New Zealanders, Austrians and Brazilians. As the women had prepared the food, the men were elected to do the dishes.

There was no curfew but I was feeling unwell and despite the good company I went to bed early.

Thursday 17th May
NAVARETTE TO NAJERA

After a restless night, I felt so ill I didn't want to get out of bed. I staggered to the bathroom, shivering, with a thumping headache, sore throat and runny nose. I kept thinking, 'I can't walk today, but I must walk today!'

At breakfast the warden came over to me and asked if I was well enough to leave. I explained the situation; we needed to go on, but I felt ill. She took me to her medicine chest, a huge box under lock and key, and gave me some pills to take four times a day for the next few days. They were large red capsules and she was convinced they would help.

There was no charge to stay at this hostel, just a donation. Ann and I felt it was worth more than the 2,000 pesetas we contributed. Thursday night pilgrims would feast well!

These kindly wardens helped us don our rucksacks and waved goodbye. It was a cool morning, but by the time the sun rose I was definitely feeling better.

Our journey took us to Najera, only 16 km away. I was glad it was a short journey. The Camino passed a cemetery with a memorial plaque on the wall to Alice de Craemer, 1986. We wondered who she was. Some pilgrims from France explained that she was a Belgian cycling on a tandem to Santiago. They thought she had been murdered.

After about 5 km we left the main road and followed a red earth track through vineyards that spread to the horizon. We knew we were in Rioja now.

There were masses of cornflowers and daisies growing profusely among the scarlet poppies. An impressionist painting come to life.

We came to the N120 and crossed over into almond groves and vineyards. There was a shepherds hut on the path with an elevated stone beside it, known as *Poyo de Roldan* (Roland's Bench).

At Aleson we walked around the gravel pit and over a dry riverbed. On through market gardens and orchards to the outskirts of Najera. Coming into town, we crossed the ring road and wound between industrial warehouses. Dark clouds loomed overhead, thunder in the distance.

Najera means 'place between the rocks' in Arabic. It was the first town to mint Christian coins. Sandstone cliffs surrounded the town dominated by the Franciscan Santa Maria la Real monastery, which was now the pilgrim refuge.

As we crossed the bridge it began to pour with rain. We dashed to the nearest hotel. I still felt rough and needed more pills. I couldn't walk any further.

The Hotel San Fernando was a new hotel and quite comfortable, with basically furnished rooms. They had a pleasant dining room with picture windows, which looked out on the cliff side. The sandstone formations were alive with house martins, curving and diving. After a late lunch I was ready for bed.

Later in the afternoon, Ann braved the weather to get our passports stamped at the monastery. We spent the evening reading maps, sorting out gear and trying to dry clothes over the standard lamp. I opened up my emergency supply pack and ordered boiling water for a miso soup and cups of tea. After a Lemsip and another giant red 'cold cure' capsule, I got a good night's sleep.

Friday 18th May
NAJERA TO AZOFRA

We made a late start after breakfast at the hotel. It was a chilly morning and I wore my fleece jacket until the sun warmed up the day. I felt low, but plodded stubbornly onwards. According to our map the terrain was very hilly toward Santo Domingo de la Calzada.

We were ahead of schedule and thought we would do half the distance today and arrive in Santa Domingo on Saturday to spend two nights rather than the one we had booked. We had three reserved stopovers en route to receive and send mail, phone family and have a rest day. So far we had averaged 20 km a day, over rocky ground, not by choice, but because of the distance between hostels.

We left the golden sandstone cliffs behind and walked out of town by way of the steep path behind the monastery. Through pine forest for a while, we followed the Camino signs on trees and posts. Our heads down, lost in thought, we tramped onward through acres of vineyard, mile after mile.

I suddenly realized there were no yellow guide marks. The village we were supposed to see on the left wasn't there. We kept going for a while, unwilling to believe we were lost. I felt so ill. I depended on Ann as a guide. She was beginning to get the bug, too, and hadn't stayed alert.

Not a soul in sight; where were we? I spotted a figure working on the vineyard slope. I propped my rucksack and stick against an olive tree and climbed up the gully, sinking into the red clay soil at every step. The man stood, leaning on his hoe, his dark wrinkled face turned to me in amazement!

In my best Spanish I asked him for directions to the Camino.

He had a guttural accent and was impossible to understand. But he clearly shook his head; this was not the Camino!

'*Donde Camino*?' (Where is it?) I repeated.

He pointed a bony hand back towards the way we had just walked.

I told Ann the disgusting news. She headed off as I hoisted my rucksack. After a while, I realized I had forgotten my walking stick! I called and shouted but the cold had affected my voice, and I could only croak.

Ann turned the corner and was out of sight.

I returned for the stick and felt fed up, furious with her for marching on ahead when I felt so rough. Luckily, Ann turned back when she realized I wasn't trudging behind.

We came to a left-hand track over the hill, hoping this was the way.

By a vineyard with a lorry load of workers, Ann yelled 'Camino?'

'*Si,*' was the unanimous reply.

We came to a sign to Azofra. We couldn't believe we were only 6 km from Najera. Later, when we checked the map and talked to other pilgrims at the hostel, we found that we had, in fact, missed a large yellow arrow on the wall where a tractor was parked. We had done a 10 km circle in the vineyard!

Azofra refuge was attached to the church of Nuestra Senora de Los Angeles, it is mentioned as the site of a battle in 968. The building dated back to 1168.

The warden showed us a musty, damp dormitory with six bunks. I surreptitiously swapped my mattress for a dryer one on another bed.

We were leaning against the wall in the sunshine, looking down the hill when an old lady bustled up and insisted on showing us the newly restored church. She was the proud caretaker. The statue of St James, garbed as a pilgrim, topped the altar.

We sat on the seat outside the refuge and listened to the organ being played; it was beautiful. The warden, who was the organist, spoke excellent English and had spent a lot of time in the States. He felt the local authorities could do more for the pilgrims; they brought money and tourism to these remote villages. We chuckled when he said he would never stay in one of these hostels. The accommodation was poor, and little was spent on improvements.

It was a lovely sunny afternoon. I did the usual sock wash and hung a few things out to air. We walked down into the village; the houses were brimming with flowerboxes and climbing roses that appeared to grow out of cracks in the pavement. A little restaurant with a 'Peregrino' (pilgrim) menu posted outside tempted us in. We sat by a window shaded by lace curtains and ordered delicious fresh trout for lunch. A shop was open and we bought vegetables to make soup for supper. I strolled down later and stocked up for tomorrow's lunch. Ann was coming down with my malady and felt like death.

Working in the small kitchen that evening was not easy; other pilgrims had arrived. The New Zealand family (who we had met way back on the track) were such fun. Mum was a teacher and had withdrawn her two daughters, aged nine and thirteen, from school for six months to travel in Europe and walk the Camino. She felt they could learn more on this trip than from six months of school. There were also two Brazilians and an annoying middle-aged Dutch couple in our dorm. I politely waited for the German ladies to prepare their supper and put on my vegetable hotpot.

Every night between 7.00–9.00 p.m. Spanish time I switched on my mobile phone. My son would ring to hear how we were doing and where we were. I gave him a detailed map of the route prior to departure, which I wished I had kept as it showed surrounding towns and villages over a wide area. All we had was the Camino map.

Sure enough at 7.00 p.m. the phone rang. We were at the kitchen table eating soup with our fellow pilgrims.

The Dutchman went mad, thumped the table and yelled arrogantly, 'We came here to escape phones; we don't want to hear phones ringing. Pilgrims shouldn't have phones!'

I had to go outside. It wasn't Stuart, my son; it was Ann's sister, who planned to join us in Leon. I went back inside and carried on eating my soup, avoiding the furious glances of the red-faced Dutchman. Ann returned the phone and blow me down, it rang again! This time it was Stuart.

The Dutchman went berserk, smashed his plate in the sink and threw his silverware. We endured this strange couple at close range in the dormitory. It was a small room and we opened the window. They slammed it closed. I said nothing, but the Brazilian boys came in to bed and opened it again. The Dutchman slammed it closed.

The Brazilians wouldn't tolerate this nonsense and yelled at him in Spanish. They opened the window even wider and threatened him if he shut it again.

I lay with my sleeping bag over my head.

After half an hour, the Dutchman roared out of the room, dragging his mattress with him, and slept on the kitchen floor. His wife stayed safely in her bunk.

At about 2.00 a.m., Ann was overcome with coughing and choking. She went into the hallway to cough in private. Needless to say, this woke the kitchen sleeper. Alarmed, Ann huddled in the bathroom, afraid she would be murdered!

Saturday 19th May
AZOFRA TO SANTO DOMINGO DE LA CALZADA

The Dutchman and his wife left at dawn. There was no '*Bon Camino*' greeting. He stormed into the bedroom, flung his mattress back on the bunk and was gone. Relieved, we rustled away with our packing (we stowed everything in plastic bags, to keep dry in case of rain).

The Brazilians leapt off the top bunks, waved and bounced down the hill, chattering happily. At 7.00 a.m. Ann and I and the New Zealand family strolled to the Peregrino restaurant for breakfast. A treat this morning: freshly squeezed orange juice with hot *tostada* and coffee. Ann felt groggy and I felt better. We chatted over breakfast to the New Zealanders.

They didn't carry sleeping bags, but showed us a sheet with a pillowcase top; they used this over the mattresses and pillows. If they were cold they slept in their thermal underwear. We liked the sheet idea and wondered if the bedding in the hostels had given us our cold germs.

We headed for Santo Domingo de la Calzada. Between Azofra and Alesanco we came to a twelfth-century Muslim boundary stone which had been converted to a cross. The guide warned us the authentic pilgrims' route is difficult to follow at times as the path crossed cultivated land. We walked through vineyards and wheat fields with few flowers and little birdsong. I suspect a lot of crop spraying had taken place here.

We met a young man from Brazil, Ernae, an engineer. He was soul-searching and hoped the walk would help him become a better man! Ann and I had trouble drawing breath, never mind soul-searching! We stopped to rest under laden almond trees.

The path ran parallel to the road into Santo Domingo and as it disappeared into the wheat field, we decided to walk on the main N120 for the last few kilometres. It was a very busy road and it was difficult to find shelter for lunch. Finally we saw some huge drainage pipes on the verge and propped our rucksacks against them to make a seat. Passing car drivers waved and sounded their horns. This cheered us enough to strut into Santo Domingo.

We followed the pilgrim signs to the convent, The Monasterio de la Encarnacion. We entered through imposing medieval doors into a dark courtyard.

In a cubicle sat two nuns on high stools at a tall desk, like a scene from *Jane Eyre*. We gave them our names, addresses and passport numbers, which they meticulously printed in pen and ink in a large bound book. They asked our ages, smiled and whispered to each other and then told us in English they thought we were well preserved for our years!

Ann felt dreadful; she just wanted to lie down. A novice escorted us to the dormitory. This little wisp of a nun opened the massive carved doors and led us upstairs. Ann collapsed onto the bottom bunk and I decided to practise getting up and down from the top bunk as niftily as possible.

We added our boots to the row on the balcony; no boots were allowed on the polished convent floors. I looked over the balcony to the courtyard below, with a rose garden on one side and pine trees on the other. Nuns sat on stools under the trees with enamel bowls and jugs of water attending pilgrims' feet. I shed a tear at the symbolic beauty of the scene.

Our feet were surviving well. We had developed a ritual of using talcum powder and wearing liners under our socks. So far this worked. Every evening I followed my chiropodist's advice and rubbed in after sun lotion to cool my feet down. The showers and bathrooms were downstairs.

The thought of having to get up in the night, climb down from my bunk go down the staircase, through the courtyard and then open the massive carved door to get to the loo caused my bladder to cringe in terror. The showers were in a new annex off the courtyard, beautifully tiled and immaculately clean.

I decided to do some laundry. One of the shower room doors was open; a girl sprawled on the floor in the shower basin with her head hanging over the side. Her eyes were closed and the shower steamed full blast. I thought she must have fallen, and was about to shout for help when she jumped up.

'Today I have reached over the 1,000 kilometres in my walk,' she explained. 'I am exhausted. I have walked from Le Puy; it was wonderful just to lie here with the water refreshing me. I hope you will understand.'

This frail-looking French girl had over 500 km more to Santiago. Our achievement of 183 km to date was nothing. Humbled, I took the washing out to the rose garden to dry in the sun and savoured the smell of the blooms mingled with pine.

Behind the rose garden was a modern office building. I could see a nun working at a computer. A different world from this side of the courtyard. Young novices scurried back and forth to the kitchen with pine logs from a pile in the corner of the yard.

We took a late afternoon stroll to the cathedral. When I pushed open the door, a rooster crowed stridently. I couldn't understand where the sound came from until I read the legend of the 'Hanged Innocent'.

A family of German pilgrims (father, mother, and son) making their way towards Compostela spent the night in Santo Domingo de la Calzada. When the innkeeper's daughter propositioned the son, he spurned her (he was, after all, on a pilgrimage). She took her revenge by convincing a friend to hide some of the church silver in the young man's pack. The next day she notified the authorities. They arrested the pilgrims and found the silver. As a result, they hung the young man for theft. In medieval times executed criminals were left on the gibbet to rot as a vivid warning of the wages of sin. The parents continued to Compostela and on their way home came again to Santo Domingo de la Calzada. Sick at heart, they approached the gibbet, where, to their astonishment, their son cheerfully greeted them, explaining that St James – or, in some versions, Santo Domingo – kept him alive by supporting his weight the whole time. Miracle! The parents ran to inform the city official that their son was still alive. The official, who was roasting chickens for dinner, scoffed at their news, retorting that their son was as alive as his roasting chickens. Whereupon the chickens reincorporated themselves, feathers and all, and flew cackling away. A piece of the gibbet is displayed high in the cathedral transept over Santo Domingo's tomb. The chickens that cackle from their coop in the west transept of the cathedral are – legend has it – descendants of the resuscitated roasters *(Gitlitz and Davidson, 2000:154).*

To commemorate this miracle, a Gothic carved niche with a Renaissance grille decorates the west wall of the cathedral, which is called the *gallinero* (or chicken coop) and which contains a pair of live white chickens, a rooster and a hen.

St Dominic was born in the nearby village. He was rejected by the monastery and became a Benedictine hermit in the town that now bears his name. He devoted his life to helping pilgrims on their way to Santiago. In 1044 he built a pilgrims' bridge over the River Oja. He also built a pilgrim hostel, a hospital and a stretch of road from Najera. When Alfonso VI took possession of Rioja in 1076 he gave his unconditional support to St Dominic, as Alfonso believed in the basic structure of a city, roads, bridges, et cetera. In 1109 St Dominic died and was buried in the town and around his tomb arose the city of Santo Domingo.

We had booked into the Parador at Santo Domingo for the following day. The Parador is the original twelfth-century hospital, which sheltered pilgrims to Santiago. Now it was magnificently restored into a luxurious stately hotel. There was a wedding and the square outside the Cathedral was packed with onlookers applauding the bride and groom. We took a side street and found a café. Bente and Josef were sitting at one of the outside tables. They were staying at the monastery opposite the convent. We joined them for dinner, washed down with a bottle of good red Rioja. The little side street led into a paved walkway with benches. We sat in the evening sun and nodded off until the shops opened! We then stocked up with water and tissues. Back at the convent, Ann felt much worse and crashed into bed. I went down to the kitchen to boil water for a Lemsip. The huge stone fireplace was ablaze with logs. Pilgrims sat round the long table having supper and drinking coffee. The candlelight and fire were cosy; upstairs it was cold. I closed the balcony window and decided to wear thermals for the night.

Sunday 20th May
SANTO DOMINGO DE LA CALZADA

I developed a cough, which disturbed the sleepers in the dormitory. At 5.00 a.m., I gingerly manoeuvred myself out of the bunk down the stone staircase, opened the old door and fumbled along the draughty corridor to the shower room and toilet.

Early in the morning we crawled over to the Parador. Perhaps they would allow us to take our room earlier than usual. The imposing lobby featured Gothic arches, stone pillars and a moulded wooden ceiling. The receptionist was very amicable and said we could have our room immediately. It was only just 8.00 a.m. We were thrilled. It would give us twenty-four hours to pamper ourselves and nurse our colds.

A parcel I had mailed from the Isle of Man was waiting for me, containing a week's supply of vitamin pills, glucose tablets, a film, my Wildlife Trust T-shirt, six more teabags and moisturizing lotion.

Our room was delightful. There was a roof garden, a courtyard and a sumptuous lounge with padded armchairs as soft as feather beds. We wallowed in the bathroom, with its scented soap and cloud-fluffy towels. Refreshed, I faxed a mileage update to the Wildlife Trust.

It was Confirmation Sunday at the cathedral. The hotel was a hive of industry catering for the big family groups. The remnants of yesterday's wedding were swept away and the banqueting hall had a new look. The tables were spread with silverware, crystal and sedate floral bouquets sparkled under the chandeliers. The square outside the cathedral was packed with families in their finery; the girls in white like little brides, and the boys in navy sailor suits with white soutache braid.

We treated ourselves to a grand lunch in the restaurant and collapsed on our beds afterwards for a snooze.

I was awakened by a telephone call from my daughter in California, who was eager to hear of our adventures. My granddaughter, Molly, had given a talk to her school assembly about my walk to raise money for Manx Wildlife.

'When I told them how many kilometres you were going to walk, nobody said anything. Do you know how many miles that is?' she said, 'It's a long way, and she's very old.'

Thank you, Molly! She laughed when I told her how Ann threw her clothes away and when we couldn't find a bush quickly enough we wet our pants!

'I can't tell assembly that, Granny, that's gross!'

When the crowds dwindled in early evening we took another look at the cathedral. As we walked once more through the great door, the 'cock-a-doodle-doo' recording was set off.

There were no live chickens in the *gallinero*. Perhaps on a weekend of confirmations and a wedding, it would have been too much for them and the recording was put into motion for the occasion!

We took a closer look at St Dominic's tomb. Scenes from the saint's life were carved along the side of his monument.

> They recount several miracles attributed to him, including the 'hanged innocent' miracle. In other scenes Domingo revives an official killed working on the Oja bridge, is mistreated by neighbours who feel his building encroaches on their rights, welcomes grateful prisoners released through his intercession, distributes charity, revives the dead son of a pilgrim couple, and has heaven punish the shepherd who destroyed his garden. (Gitlitz and Davidson, 2000:157).

The graceful bell tower is known locally as *'la moza de la Rioja'* ('the young woman of La Rioja').

We strolled through the old town where shops were filled with rooster images, from brightly painted 'Made in China' bric-a-brac to expensive silver and gold jewellery. Enjoyed a pot of tea at the hotel and had an early night. We already felt one hundred per cent better!

Monday 21st May
SANTO DOMINGO DE LA CALZADA TO SAN JUAN DE ORTEGA

As soon as the Parador buffet breakfast was set out at 7.00 a.m., we promptly sampled the goodies. We stocked up with a doggy bag for lunch and popped some fruit in our pockets! My safari jacket was bulging and I looked as if I had a size sixty bust!

We went to reception and settled the bill, grateful for the thirty-five per cent off for pensioners! A fax had arrived overnight with news from the Wildlife Trust. Sponsorship money so far: over £1,500.

After yesterday's bustle the streets were quiet and still as I walked through the main square. The impressive town hall stretched along one side, with galleries and arches emblazoned with banners and crests. The post office opened at 8.00 a.m. and I mailed a parcel back home. They gave me their full attention; they must be used to wittering pilgrims. I wondered if a filthy pair of trousers and a T-shirt was worth all this form filling and official stamping.

Back at the Parador, the receptionist studied our map and explained there wasn't a bus to the Camino route nearby. The Camino wove its way around the main N120, but there was no bus stop until Belorado, after which was a 12 km walk along the main road to Redecilla. We decided to take a taxi ride for 2,000 pesetas, which would drop us at Espinosa.

On the way out of the city we crossed the twenty-four arch bridge over the River Oja built by St Dominic, which had been spoiled by hideous modern cement parapets. 6 km out of Santo Domingo we went through Granon, the frontier between the kingdoms of Castile and Navarre. An old Santiago guidebook claimed the Camino route from Najera to Burgos was the most arduous as it crossed the Montes De Oca, and recommended hiring a horse! That was before motorways and taxis! Taking the N120 out of Belorado we crossed the bridge over the River Tiron. A few miles on at Tosantos we saw a small church carved out of the limestone hillside, which housed a twelfth-century statue of the Virgin Mary. The taxi driver dropped us at the junction in the road before Espinosa. We crossed the N120 and walked into the deserted hamlet.

Three pilgrims were drinking coffee outside a small bar, their bikes propped against a rickety brick wall.

'Camino?' we said.

They pointed to the path behind the bar. We followed dim yellow signs through the abandoned houses and the ramshackle village. Marigolds and daisies grew amongst the weeds around doors and in derelict gardens. We climbed a stoney track and then downhill to Villafranca Montes de Oca. Alongside the path before the village, was a ruined chapel built of stone, which was entered through a horseshoe arch. It was all that remained of a tenth-century monastery. The church had a bell tower with one large and one small bell. The small one had been turned upside down, but I couldn't find the reason for this. The font was made of a giant shell from the Philippines.

We faced 12 km of way marked forest without a village until we reached San Juan de Ortega. The guidebook read:

>…this was in medieval times the most feared stretch of the pilgrim's route; due to the steepness, dense undergrowth and harsh climate, above all, because it was infested with bloodthirsty bandits who would rob and murder passing pilgrims. (Lozano, 1999)

We climbed through pines into an oak woodland, then onto heather moorland as we ascended into the Montes de Oca. The heather was huge and shrub-like; pinky mauve and white in colour, it stretched around us in great banks. There were a lot of wild flowers. A lily flower, a bright blue flower, and a delicate little white rose were unfamiliar. The gold of broom and gorse added more colour. Snow gleamed on the distant mountains. The track was stony and rugged. We continued to climb through the pine forest.

We met Bente and Jacob and Eloise, the French girl from Le Puy. They were picnicking by a monument to a group of local people executed in the Spanish Civil War.

It was late afternoon when we left the forest track and arrived at San Juan de Ortega in the heart of the Montes de Oca. It was like entering a film set. The monastery with great wrought iron ornamental gates, adjacent to the Romanesque church, is now a restored pilgrims' hostel. Work was in progress on the monastery and scaffolding supported temporary roofing.

The old parish priest greeted us and we waited in the stone arched hallway while he registered and stamped our passports. We were informed that Mass would be held at 6.00 p.m., followed by a supper of garlic soup served in the monastery.

The refuge dormitory was a draughty stone hall that slept eighty pilgrims. The conditions were primitive; the mattresses on the beds were wet from the leaking roof, there was one shower and only cold water. The Confraternity of Saint James guidebook stated the San Juan de Ortega refuge had 'somewhat unhygienic conditions'!

To be frank, it was awful, but we had no alternative as the next refuge was 13 km away. Despite the cold water, I had to have a shower. I walked in with my towel to find Josef standing there stark naked; there was no curtain or door! We washed our underwear in the village fountain; there was no washing line. Pilgrims draped their wet clothes on the trees and bushes.

There was a small bar by the monastery. We scouted around to find food and water and met the New Zealand family on the same mission. The café served omelettes and salad. We had a glass of beer and chatted.

The family had walked all the way. Dad and the girls were in fine form and enjoying every minute. Ann and I suspected Mum was fed up having to do all the washing and food organization.

We decided to miss the service. Our colds were not completely cured and we wanted to lie down in the sunshine; the thought of wet beds tonight was depressing.

Josef came into the bar and purchased two bottles of wine. 'If I'm having the soup,' he said, 'I've got to wash it down with something.'

We watched the priest carry the bucket of soup into the monastery; it looked white and frothy with orange globules floating on top. Wet beds and garlic breath tonight; what an unpleasant thought.

San Juan was born in 1080, in a nearby hamlet. He became St Dominic's principal disciple, building churches, hospitals, roads and bridges. After St Dominic's death, he survived a shipwreck on the way home from Jerusalem, and vowed to dedicate the rest of his life to helping pilgrims. He cleared a way through the wilderness known as Ortega (meaning 'nettle') and founded an Augustinian monastery. St John became the patron saint of childless women.

> The reason is that when his tomb was opened, there was a pleasant odor, and out flew a swarm of white bees, which were interpreted to be the souls of unborn children that the Saint was keeping safe pending their incarnation in the wombs of the faithful. Among the women who trekked to the site was Isabel la Catolica, childless queen of Castilla, who came to the monastery to pray for a son and heir. She took home an arm from the monastery's crucifix as a souvenir. When at last she conceived she named the boy Juan. After his death she came again to pray, and when her next child was born, she named her Juana. (Gitlitz and Davidson, 2000:168)

In gratitude to St John, Isabel had the chapel rebuilt in a sumptuous style. Pillar carvings show a well-endowed San Juan.

Josef came into the church to find me looking at the figure and remarked, 'I thought you had seen enough phalli for one day!'

St John's tomb is intricately carved with scenes from his life. A carving of the Annunciation is upon a nearby pillar. Each equinox (March 21st and September 22nd) at precisely 5.00 p.m. solar time, a single shaft of sunlight illuminates the figure of Mary, which some observers believe is the light of the Holy Ghost descending upon the Virgin's belly. This was an unforgettable church, steeped in legend and mystery.

The dormitory was cold and damp. You could see the sky through the roof and the windows didn't shut properly. What a change from the Parador to this. We worried that our colds might become worse rather than better. Despite misgivings, I slept well. We got up at 5.00 a.m. and were ready to move out at 5.30 a.m. It was still dark when we left.

Tuesday 22nd May
SAN JUAN DE ORTEGA TO BURGOS

So glad to leave the damp dirty refuge and be out in the fresh air. Today we planned to walk to Burgos, the capital city of northern Spain. I pinned my wet towel and socks to my rucksack to dry. The sun came up strongly and burned off the dew. There are three routes into Burgos; we chose the one across the Sierra, well away from the main roads. The dusty track led us through a now derelict village called Agés with an old fountain.

> In 1052 King Garcia el de Najera (Navarra) gave the village to the monastery of Santa Maria la Real in Najera. A marker at the entrance to the church says that he was buried here after his brother Fernando I of Castilla killed him in the September 15th, 1054, battle of Atapuerca, halfway between the two towns. The site is known locally as Fin de Rey (Kings End)…
> In the early Middle Ages it (Agés) was large enough to have a small Jewish community. (Gitlitz and Davidson, 2000:171)

Sad to think we all become derelict eventually. This trip was supposed to help us fight back, but the dereliction was winning. We crossed a little one-arched bridge that was the work of San Juan of Ortega.

The next village was Atapuerca where there was a bar open for coffee. All they had to eat were floury white lumps of bread. I asked for *marmelada* and the owner handed me the jar her children were using for their own breakfast as they sat at a table getting ready for school.

The Sierra de Atapuerca was honeycombed with caves. In 1992 some prehistoric remains were found here which are so old that 'Atapuerca man' is possibly the earliest example of *Homo sapiens* in Europe.

Our blistered feet and cranky knees felt like relics. We climbed out of the village, through woodland and into the sierra. The wild flowers were beautiful, meadows full of orchids, the lily flower, and banks of broom. There were varieties of orchids in profusion: bee-orchids, twayblades and a lovely cream speckled one unfamiliar to me. We were in undulating meadowland and walked through a large herd of cows with their calves; they had sleek, shiny coats, and their neck bells clanged as they grazed on the lush grass. The farmer watched us, his Alsatian dog and pups at his feet. They did not stir as we walked by, probably used to sweating red-faced pilgrims.

We arrived at the sleepy hamlet of Cardenuela. Ann was way ahead of me; I kept stopping and picking flowers to press in my travel diary. She was sitting on a seat outside a little bar and had ordered a *tortilla baguette*, which we shared – delicious. We had a fresh orange juice and enjoyed a break in the shade. It was very, very hot. We were now on the gravel track heading for Villafria and had to cross the busy motorway. The tarmac was melting in the heat. We looked down on Villafria with its massive church and crawled wearily along the road towards Burgos.

Following the motorway and the main road, we had another 4 km to the city. We decided to take the bus into the centre of Burgos and thus avoid the suburbs and traffic. We enquired at the nearby hotel about buses.

The receptionist directed us to a caravan site, a short block away. 'Bus soon,' she said.

We waited in the sun for nearly an hour. Ann wondered if we had misunderstood her Spanglish. We returned to the hotel to ask if they would ring for a taxi.

The receptionist waved her arms, 'Bus now, hurry!'

Halfway back to the stop, we saw the bus and ran like mad things. Passengers helped us throw our rucksacks aboard. Ann leaned back with a sigh, uncaring about our destination. I watched the Centro Ciudad signs and made a quick decision to jump off the bus when we stopped at the corner by the bridge.

There were several signs for hotels. The first one we headed for was full; the second a four-star, also *completo*.

The city was packed with people and the heat was unbearable. The refuge was on the far bank of the river, about 4 km out of the city. We couldn't make it that far as we had already walked 24 km. We tramped into the old part of town and followed directions to a hotel; we circled around, couldn't find the place. We were getting desperate; I was unable to take another step! Ann begged me to stop.

We sat in the shade beneath a tree by the river; perhaps we could sleep here on the bench? I suggested we find a taxi to take us to a hotel, any hotel, but we hadn't seen anything resembling a taxi. We crawled back to the bus stop, which was in a tourist area, and asked again.

We were redirected back into the old town to a two-star hotel in a quiet square. The owner told us that all the rooms had been taken over by the Russian Ballet Company, which was performing that week in Burgos. Tonight was the last night. They were having a big party at the hotel.

He had one small room, but it would be very noisy and the party would probably go on all night. We didn't care, any room would do, anywhere! We sidled into the cosy little cupboard, just large enough for two beds and our rucksacks.

We unrolled our sleeping bags to air; they were still wet from the San Juan refuge. Ann's cold bothered her and she needed to rest. We showered and napped for a while.

We awoke hungry and thirsty so ventured out again in the evening. The heat had not dissipated with the setting sun; it was the hottest May on record for northern Spain.

We didn't feel like going far and walked to a huge old restaurant with brass-edged counters, high ceilings and old lamps. There was a *tapas* bar that stretched the length of the place with an amazing variety of snacks. We filled plates and sat down drooling. They looked better than they tasted. We were too tired to care, and nibbled till we were full!

Burgos was a wonderful city. We planned to spend the next morning exploring before moving on. Back at the hostel we went straight to sleep, exhausted. I heard sporadic screams and laughter in the background – the Russian Ballet Company was enjoying its party, but it didn't bother me in the least.

Wednesday 23rd May
BURGOS TO SAHAGUN

We were up early. Ann felt much better. We went down to the restaurant for breakfast. The door was locked and we were told to come back at 7.00 a.m. We jostled for the lift to our floor with emaciated creatures from the Russian ballet; they pirouetted along the corridors, gauzy shirts and tight jeans revealed their taut muscles. Bony Eastern European faces contrasted with our lumpen middle age.

We packed our rucksacks and took time to look at the map. We had booked a room at the hotel in Leon, the Hostal San Marcos Parador, a grand place, and the high spot luxury of our tour. We must arrive by Saturday the 27th. My friend Barbara, from Washington, would meet us there. Ann's sisters and friend would arrive in Leon on the 29th. Son Stuart said he would join us somewhere on the route and would walk with us into Leon. We knew we could not make it by the 27th if we walked every step of the way. We would be pushed for time. Therefore we planned to bus to Palencia which would eliminate several miles.

We were finally ushered in for breakfast, all very basic with numbered tables. We had a quick coffee, pocketed some rolls, and left our rucksacks behind the reception desk for a few hours while we explored the city.

Due to the climatic extremes of Burgos, cold winters, and long dry summers, it was not a prolific agricultural area, and focused from its beginning on commercial ventures. It became a cosmopolitan town where Muslims, Jews and Christians traded together, sometimes peacefully.

It was a lovely sunny morning as we walked to the cathedral. It dominates the city; a magnificent building with Gothic towers, the first stones of which were laid in 1221 by Fernando III. The work on the cathedral lasted until the sixteenth-century. It is considered one of the most artistic monuments in Spain.

One of the cathedral's Gothic towers was scaffolded for restoration work. Inside was awe-inspiring. A statue of St James graced the altar and in the Capilla de Santiago (Chapel of St James) another sixteenth-century statue dominated: St James the Moor-slayer!

We walked back through Plaza Santa Maria beneath the great arch and along the riverbank flanked with old trees cut back to replicate arches. We retraced our steps, crossed over the bridge and found our way to the bus station. The only destination listed on the Camino route was Sahagun.

We had forty-five minutes to get back to the hostel, collect our rucksacks and sticks, and return to the bus station for the Sahagun bus. We stopped at a little kiosk shop and bought some fruit, biscuits and chocolate. No one knew the departure bay for Sahagun and we rushed like anxious chickens from one stop to another. We were glad we had chosen to ride the bus as the route was flat and boring. Pilgrims walked in groups alongside the road, breathing in diesel fumes and covered with dust. We could see the Camino path followed the main road for most of the journey.

I had read that a lot of pilgrims take the train from Fromista to Sahagun for this very reason. I heard also that Sahagun was a dreary commercial town. The approach by bus into the town was discouraging: tawdry and run down. We expected the worst but were to be pleasantly surprised. The refuge in the guidebook was not recommended so we looked for somewhere to stay.

It was early afternoon and very hot. We stopped at a bar for two cold orange drinks. The young girl behind the bar charged us twice as much as we normally paid. I questioned it and she tossed her head and turned away. Ann moaned about the pilgrim tourist rip-off, which was actually uncommon throughout northern Spain. But Ann moans a lot: about her feet, about food, about the heat… a cheerful companion!

We walked up the street to the top of the hill where we saw a hotel with a hanging sign; Hostel Alfonso VI. As we walked in, the place appeared clean and modern, but there was no reception area. The dining room was directly off the lobby, and was full of locals having lunch. The owner came out of the kitchen, took off his apron and showed us to an upstairs room. The room was en suite. It was fresh and comfortable. The food in the dining room looked and smelled delicious. We opted to have lunch immediately.

Later that afternoon we saw a maid hanging laundry on drying racks on the roof. We found some space on the line and hung our tatty underwear to dry in the warm sun.

Early evening we strolled down the hill to the centre of town. It was an ancient world! A great Gothic arch led us into a plaza with gardens fronting a Moorish church which had seventeen arched towers on each of its four sides.

The church housed a museum of treasures. Kings of Leon and Castille, Alfonso VI and two popes are buried here. There were gold and silver ornaments and ornate statues. It was beyond belief that we had been told this town was dreary! It was steeped in history.

The pilgrim refuge next to the church in the town centre looked very nice and well-organized. Perhaps this was new since the guidebook was written? Sahagun was once the seat of the most powerful Benedictine monastery in Spain. All that remained was the arch of the gateway and belfry. The walls of this once Christian monastery were covered in fine Moorish carving. Restoration work was ongoing.

Sahagun produced many ecclesiastical dignitaries. Aided by royal favours and endowments from Alfonso VI and his successors, Sahagun became the most powerful monastery on the pilgrim's route. Records show that in 1085 there were inhabitants from nine different countries. The Centre for Studies into the Pilgrims' Route to Santiago is also here.

A group of German pilgrims were in the church with us, and the warden offered to take everyone up to the Peregrina Convent, which was normally closed. She took a ring of massive keys and we followed her up the hill. One of the German pilgrims was blind; nevertheless he kept up with the group by holding onto the shoulder of the person in front. The guide opened the door to the chapel. The painting in the apse of two monks embracing in penitential reverence commemorated the reconciliation between the Franciscan and Benedictine orders.

We had enjoyed our time in ancient Sahagun. It was a magnificent town.

Back at the hostel we collected our laundry and strung a line across the window to catch the last of the sun. I managed to get the hostel owner to make us some tea and we picnicked in our room. I was falling asleep when the mobile rang. It was Stuart, who said he was definitely coming at the weekend and would fly from Brussels to Madrid and take a coach up to Leon.

Thursday 24th May
SAHAGUN TO CALZADILLA HERMANILLOS

We gathered our laundry and stuffed it in our bags. Coffee and madelaines at the hostel and we were off just after 7.00 a.m. The way out of Sahagun led over the Puente de Canto (The Singing Bridge), which crossed the River Cea.

We walked downhill from the hostel as a team of French cyclists, wearing tight biking shorts, their muscular legs pumping away, shouted '*Bon Camino*.'

Our hearts fluttered as they sped along.

The track followed the road for about 5 km; we went through a tunnel under the N120. At this point there was a choice of two routes. We decided to take the old pilgrim road to Calzadilla de Hermanillos, which, according to the guidebook, had a spacious and comfortable refuge. The path was a compacted earth track, flanked either side by poplars; this was built by the regional government for general use, and ran all the way to Mansilla de las Mulas. I felt the hard-baked earth track and the occasional sharp stone through the soles of my boots; my feet were now blistered, with open sores and throbbing heels.

A miraculous incident that happened on this route is recounted in *The History of Charlemagne and Roland*, written in the twelfth-century:

> ...they came across the Saracens in the land known as Campos, beside the Cea, in some fields in a very fertile, flat place where, afterwards, upon Charlemagne's orders and with his help, the great and excellent Basilica of the Holy Martyrs Facundo and Primitivo was built. Some Christian soldiers were conscientiously preparing their weapons the night before

the battle and thrust them upright into the ground, in front of the camp: that is to say, in the fields beside the river. When dawn broke the next day, those who were to receive the honour of martyrdom for their faith in God found their lances covered in bark and with leafy branches. More amazed than can be described, and attributing such a miracle to the divine power of the Lord, they cut them down to the ground and from the buried roots the great woods we see there today grew up, as many of the lances had ash shafts. (Lozano, 1999)

No fewer than 40,000 Christians were killed in the battle beside the Cea.

We by passed the village of Calzada and moved off the new track to take a path through flat farmland, mostly oats and barley. There were banks of wild lavender, reeds and iris surrounding wetland areas where frogs croaked and birds sang. Great flocks of little light brown birds with lime green bellies dipped and dived in a sea of viridian grasses. I had seen the same birds in Pamplona. I think they were from the leaf warbler family. Coots swam and gossiped on one pond. There was a hum of wildlife all around us; crickets in the meadow banks and constant birdsong. There was no one in sight along this old route. We thought we had detoured somehow as it took longer to reach the Coruna–Leon railway crossing than the map indicated. The track became monotonous clay-like ground with some sand and stone.

It was midday and the sun was scorching. Ahead we saw a few trees and a wooded area. This was our goal for a lunch break. Ann forged ahead and was sprawled out under a tree; she looked like a beached whale, inert and semi-conscious.

There is a story told of two travellers in this area who found the corpse of a dead pilgrim half-eaten by wolves. 'Well, here goes another dead pilgrim!' I thought as I hobbled up to her prostrate form.

The trees were thorn bushes and did not afford much shade but were dense enough to get some relief from the sun. The ground was covered with little yellow daisies with ochre-coloured dots in the centre. There were also patches of the lily-like flower; I thought they were Asphodelus. We enjoyed a good picnic lunch: pâté, cheese and pears washed down with orange juice. Our sacks were a good deal lighter; we'd pretty much eaten everything! Leaving the remains of our bread under the thorn bush for the creatures to enjoy, we pulled on our rucksacks and started walking.

We could hear a train whistle close by on the Leon line, with piercing blasts. We turned.

'Perhaps there is something on the line,' Ann said.

It was a small train: only two carriages. Leaning from the engine cab were two drivers. They shouted and waved at us. To our astonishment, there were several passengers waving from the windows as well.

'*Bravo! Bravo!*' they shouted. '*Bon Camino, Bon Camino.*'

We waved back, feeling special and heroic. 'Well, there we are, our fifteen minutes of fame.'

We strode on, our backs straight, feeling cheerful in spite of the dense undergrowth, and came to a huge farm, the first building for 10 km. There were two Roman milestones and the original paving stones of the Calzada de los Peregrinos – the Pilgrims Road. We smelled thyme that we crushed with our boots, as we tramped through a field with swathes of seeding pink grasses. There were thick red-stalked ferns with dense fronds and patches of the bright yellow daisy.

We arrived at the sleepy adobe village of Calzadilla Hermanillos. Everywhere was locked up; it was siesta time. The houses were rustic, made of clay and straw. On the church tower, storks rested in an untidy bundle of sticks. Two nestlings peered over the edge; it was a long drop to the grass below.

The houses were amazing: elaborate wooden shutters, some with wrought iron grilles; they looked centuries old. But, incongruously, they had water and electricity meters attached to the tan mud walls and some had television aerials.

We found the refuge and a young American girl greeted us; she was walking back from Santiago to Roncesvalles. As we unpacked she went off to the warden's house to tell her of the arrival of more pilgrims. We registered and our passports were once again stamped; they now looked quite impressive with different designs and logos from each port of call. It cost us 300 pesetas each for the night's stay – just over £1.

It was a small refuge, but organized and clean. It was described in the guidebook as spacious. We hadn't yet found a refuge of which the details were correct. There was a tiny kitchen that had a washing machine. We purchased a tablet of washing powder for 250 pesetas.

Another pilgrim, a middle-aged lady from Austria, told us that the bar at the opposite end of town would cook supper, probably not before 8.00 or 9.00 p.m., but we needed to order beforehand.

The bar was clean and modern with the usual siesta time crowd of beer and wine drinkers. They propped up the counter and gossiped and coughed in a haze of foul-smelling tobacco smoke. A chubby young woman behind the bar told us she would prepare pork chops, potatoes and salad. Maybe vegetable soup if there was time, but nothing would be served before 8.30 p.m.

As we needed fresh supplies for the next day we searched for a shop. I spotted some crates piled haphazardly outside an adobe house, indistinguishable from its neighbour's, where an old man tended his roses in the garden.

I asked him in my limited Spanish, '*Mercado no abierto?*' (The market not open?)

I struggled to understand him and I thought he said the proprietor was visiting his brother and would be back by 6.00 p.m.

We decided, 'To hell with the wash,' we would snooze away the afternoon. It was too hot to do anything. At 6.00 p.m. I returned to the shop. It was still closed. The old man leaned on his garden wall and watched me.

'*No abierto?*' I queried.

He shook his head; sometimes the owner visited his brother and didn't return until the following day!

Having struggled to understand him, I returned to a disgruntled Ann with the news that we would probably have to starve tomorrow!

A dapper young Frenchman wearing a jaunty leather hat checked in at the hostel. He asked about dinner and we sent him across the village to the bar.

Then in the warm evening air the four of us sauntered through town. We watched the bats circling, gobbling up the gnats, swooping along between the houses and soaring around the church tower.

Over dinner we discussed our reasons for making the pilgrimage. It was amazing how we managed to communicate so well, explaining and understanding in our limited Spanish, French and German. We were all very different. The Austrian lady was walking for spiritual reasons; Ann said her husband had recently been diagnosed with Alzheimer's disease and she would be tied to his care in the future and wanted this to be a time of peace to think and reflect. The Frenchman's girlfriend had left him and he hoped the walk would clear his mind and help him face the future without her. I told them how I hoped to raise a lot of money for the Wildlife Trust in the Isle of Man. Most of us were on the walk for the sheer joy of freedom from worry, to be with our own thoughts: to look backwards and forwards, to contemplate and reflect on life.

We drank beer and wine, bought milk and water from the bar owner for the next day and walked back to the refuge very happy with life and without a care in the world.

The refuge door swung open all night and the window in our cubicle didn't close properly. At lights out we couldn't find the switch. Huffing around in our nightshirts we finally located it, fiendishly concealed in the next cubicle. It was near midnight, the latest we had stayed up on our trip.

Friday 25th May
CALZADILLA HERMANILLAS TO EL BURGO RANEROS

We woke late to find the sun streaming in through the open window. Everyone had gone except the American girl, who was in the kitchen boiling up our milk! We grabbed a coffee and left by 8.00 a.m. We were unsure of the roads leading from town; the map was unclear and the directions vague.

One road would take us to Mansilla and the other to El Burgo Raneros. The Coruna railway line ran through the middle. We hailed a car.

Three smart Spanish ladies peered out at us in amazement, with our wispy hair, tattered rucksacks and heavy, muddy hiking boots. They, as so many Spanish women we had seen, were the epitome of fashionable elegance. 'Keep left and eventually you will arrive at the *pueblo* (village).'

It seemed to make sense until we came to a small narrow lane, which had a 'Prohibited' sign at the entrance. We were discussing our options when we saw the French boy in the distance. He had left the refuge an hour before us and wandered in circles. He took off his leather hat, wiped his brow and studied the maps. He wasn't prepared to take the 'Prohibited' road and decided to retrace his steps. Those Spanish ladies were familiar with the road so we resolved to follow their directions.

We stopped for a rest on a bed of thyme; there were wild sweet peas, vetch and daisies on the banks. We followed a canal for about 4 km and began to wonder if we were on the right route.

Ann climbed up the high bank on the opposite side of the canal. She saw the railway line and a village in the distance. 'Great, it's the way, keep walking!' she called and slithered down the bank.

Mud plastered her shorts and prickles had worked their way into her socks. Ann was afraid to unlace her boots because of a swollen toe she thought had become infected.

The walk had taken a toll on our feet. We had not anticipated the severity of the problems.

We emerged by a reservoir that led us out onto the road. At last a sign to El Burgo Raneros. As we walked towards the village, a new silver-grey Mercedes pulled up and the driver, an attractive middle-aged Spaniard, offered us a lift.

I whispered to Ann, 'No,' but she was already taking her rucksack off and thanking him.

'I am the local priest,' he explained, and opened the boot for our packs. His robes and hat were in there, neatly folded. How could a priest be so affluent?

I tugged on Ann's arm and hissed, 'I don't believe him.' I was still not convinced, but Ann was already sitting in the back seat.

He took us to Raneros, which was only 2 km away and dropped us by the bar opposite the refuge, which wouldn't open until 2.00 p.m. We sat in the shade and had cold beers, a potato tortilla and bread. There were several pilgrims waiting for the refuge to open. We walked down to the little village shop; it was well stocked with fresh vegetables and fruit. We decided to prepare our own evening meal and buy rice and vegetables for a risotto.

This one-street town was deserted; it was siesta. The houses were nearly all adobe and so was the refuge. However, the guide was almost right this time. To quote:

> This excellent Domenico Laffi municipal refuge, featuring thirty-six bunk beds, has magnificent facilities and ranks one of the most elegant and authentic refuges on the Pilgrim route. (Lozano, 1999)

It was one of the nicest we had encountered, but magnificent and elegant? No! It was of clay and straw with open beams and a fireplace, basic and clean. It was currently run by a volunteer, a German girl. Today was her last day.

After registering we sat outside for a while to do some writing, when Richard and Russ arrived, followed by Claude, a French man we had first met walking from Irache.

We were delighted to see them and agreed to make a communal evening meal. They would bring the wine and dessert. Claude had found a butcher to cut him a steak and he planned to prepare it with salad. He was seventy-two years old and immaculate, austere and disciplined. No sooner had he arrived at the hostel than his boots were cleaned, his meal was on the stove, his wash was on the line and he had showered and shaved. All this while we were fumbling around with our rucksacks and sorting out our possessions!

The warden asked if she could join us for supper if she made percolated coffee for everyone. She told me I could use the olive oil or anything else I could find in the kitchen. We needed to slip back to the shop to stock up on a few more vegetables!

We took our notebooks and pens and ambled through the village. We passed the old church with two storks nesting on the roof and house martins perched on the wrought iron gates. On the edge of the town there was a large pond. We walked round listening to the frogs croaking and jumping in the grass. I had never seen so many frogs. We tossed stones into the reeds and hundreds of them jumped up in fear. Centuries ago, the village merchants sold frogs to the nearby towns.

There were coots on the water and yellow iris on the bank. Birds swooped over the reeds and bulrushes. We sat under a tree and I made a pen drawing of the pond and church tower, which rose above the adobe buildings. I longed to paint this country scene. On our way back to the hostel we stopped at the bar for a cold drink when who should walk in, resplendent in his hat and robes, but the priest who gave us a lift that morning! The village appeared to be so poor; we still can't figure that Mercedes.

The only piece of history I read about El Burgo Raneros was an extract from the *Historical Pilgrims Accounts*, dated 1673, by the Dominican Laffi (whose name has been given to this hostel):

> We sat off towards El Burgo Raneros, four leagues away and we found lodgings, but so poor that we had to sleep on the floor, as all the inhabitants of this village are shepherds and all the dwellings are straw roofed huts. (Lozano, 1999)

Not that it has changed much today!

Laffi's records for the same year in this area continually mention the swarms of locust that are destroying all the crops and the herds of wolves in such numbers that they eat the livestock night and day. In Sahagun, he said,

> …upon arriving at this place, we saw the walls covered with so many locusts that it stirred our hearts to pity to see them. In the city, the women go out into the streets and round them up and kill them with sticks. (Lozano, 1999)

We had a very sociable evening. The risotto was a great success. Russ said it was his best meal on the Camino. Claude joined us and ate his steak!

Richard and Russ taunted him in a friendly way all evening. 'We can never get rid of you, no matter how fast we walk! You are only twenty years older than we are, after all! You fast little Frenchman; what are you trying to prove?'

Everyone thought we had done well. We shamefacedly admitted to the odd bit of bussing.

There was plenty of wine and lots of risotto left, so I distributed it all round! Dessert was a huge yucky Danish-type pastry with lots of icing and jam; very sticky!

The warden wasn't in a hurry to put out the lights. She was enjoying her last night. Richard and Russ were in our dormitory on the top bunks. We spent a lot of time talking to each other about our families, wives, ex-wives, husbands and children. My eyes closed and I fell asleep with Russ's Texan drawl as a background lullaby.

Saturday 26th May
EL BURGO RANEROS TO
MANSILLA DE LAS MULAS

We made a very early start; it was dark when we left the hostel. I sat under a tree in the dusky dawn light and wrapped my feet in yards of tape. Ann's toe was infected and, as a result, she put most of her weight on her left knee and it was beginning to swell. A fine pair!

I phoned Stuart on his mobile; he was in Madrid and making his way up to Leon. We would meet him in Mansilla de las Mulas, 22 km along the Camino.

The guidebook reads, 'Be prepared; there is no shelter, no shade, no water, and no food, nothing on this stretch to Mansilla.'

We were prepared for the worst, but it wasn't as bad as we thought. We forsook the old Roman route and opted for the newer, neatly groomed one: flat and stony with compacted red earth. Passing the village pond where we sat yesterday we made our way along a poplar-lined track and limped for 10 km across a vast monotonous plateau.

The area was dotted with gullies, river tributaries called *arroyas*, seven in all. Some of these wetland areas had benches and picnic tables set out under young freshly planted poplar trees. The route was well tended by the local authorities. The guide certainly needed updating. There was a sign for potable water at one *arroya*. We wandered through the reeds and bulrushes but couldn't find the source of the water.

I now had several blisters on top of blisters and felt every stone through the soles of my boots. My feet were burning hot. I nearly trod on a hedgehog crossing the path; he blended in with the stone so well.

In between the *arroyas* there were wheat and oat fields with poppies, daisies and a few cornflowers dotted here and there. By midday the sun was very hot and we stopped to picnic under a tree by an *arroya*. The frogs croaked incessantly.

We plodded on, sighting the village of Villamarco and once again crossed the Leon–Coruna railway line. Arroya de Santa Maria was the last before reaching Mansilla de las Mulas. The valley was wooded with a gurgling stream over a rocky bed. We came to the hamlet of Reliegos, which had been an important junction in Roman times. Horrified to realize we still had 6 km to walk, we comforted each other by imagining the pounds we were losing.

'Anyway,' Ann said, 'this whole trip reminds me of sex. We are old; it takes us a lot longer, but we still get there in the end!'

Running parallel with the old Roman route, we descended to Mansilla de las Mulas on the banks of the Esla river. Passing some ugly rubbish dumps and sprawling suburbs, we reached the old quarter through the south gate, the Puerta de Santiago which had lost its arch.

Mansilla de las Mulas translated means *mano-en-silla* (hand on the saddle) *de las mulas* (of the mules). This explains the town's coat of arms emblazoned on the town hall: a hand on a saddle. Until recently, Mansilla was the centre for buying and selling horses. Cattle farmers came from as far afield as the mountains of Leon.

Very hot and tired, we followed the signs to the pilgrim refuge, which was near the church in the old part of town. A young Dutch group we had met previously greeted us warmly. They were in the kitchen preparing a mammoth fruit salad.

I complained to them about my feet and they recommended some silicone insoles, which were sold by a local pharmacy.

The hostel was old with a central courtyard. There were brightly painted murals on the walls. Richard and Claude were there. Richard slept in the courtyard, one leg propped up, his knee wrapped in an elastic support. Claude sat at a table writing postcards; he looked as fresh as a daisy, and had arrived several hours earlier. How did he do it? He had purchased a steak from the local butcher and was waiting to pan-fry it when the fruit salad makers finished in the kitchen.

We booked in for the night and saved a bunk for Stuart.

After a shower, we climbed into our bunks for a rest and fell asleep immediately, but woke abruptly when a party of Germans arrived, followed by an even noisier party of Spaniards. Siesta over, we went into the old town to explore.

Stuart drew up in a taxi as we walked down the street. It was good to see my tall young son. We took him back into the refuge with his rucksack, introduced him to the warden then set off again. The town buildings were crumbling away and topsy-turvy. Roofs had caved in, balconies were supported by timber, in some cases nothing more elaborate than a tree trunk. The main attraction was the old town walls:

> Walls. More than three-quarters of the medieval walls remain. In parts they are three metres thick. Most were built by Fernando II of Leon as part of his line of fortifications against Castilla. The construction is typical of twelfth-century fortifications in the Tierra de Campos, using the Mudejar techniques with clay, brick and rubble-work. Two gates are left... (Gitlitz and Davidson, 2000:241)

There was a modern pilgrim statue in the square. It portrayed three exhausted, reeling figures wearing their scallop shells to identify them as pilgrims. They were lying at the foot of a pillar with a cross on the top, Christ carved on one side of the cross and Mary on the other, gazing with compassion on the pilgrims at their feet.

We shopped for tomorrow's picnic and I went to the *farmacia* (pharmacy) and purchased the silicone insoles for my boots. They were like lumps of jelly. We found a bar for

71

drinks and booked dinner in their restaurant for 8.00 p.m. It was an excellent meal. We were pleasantly surprised to be ushered into a very comfortable dining room with a table set for us. Linen napkins, glasses and wine: how civilized and relaxing. I chose fresh asparagus and a delicious baked fish.

Back at the refuge, one of the wardens dragged mattresses into the hallway. It was very busy; many more pilgrims had arrived.

We saw the Australian girl we had met at the communal supper in Navarette. She and her boyfriend planned to sleep in the courtyard. One of the wardens, a Brazilian girl, administered to travellers' feet. I joined the queue. She was a six-week volunteer from Rio de Janeiro, a veterinary surgeon by profession! She assured me she cleaned the needles with antiseptic. From then on I couldn't look. The blisters on top of blisters were the ones causing the problems. All plastered up and with my new jelly soles I hoped for a better day tomorrow.

The hostel was jam-packed. A German lady in the opposite bunk asked me how old I was, as she thought we were the same age. She was three years younger; we both agreed it was tough going and envied the youngsters their 30+ km a day!

Stuart took a shower and put his clothes back on, ready for early departure. The dormitory was crowded and noisy. I donated my paracetamol to a young French boy who had a raging headache.

Fell asleep to the sounds of grunts, farts and snores!

Sunday 27th May
Mansilla de las Mulas to Leon

Bags rustled, alarms bleeped and narrow beams from pocket torches sliced across the bunks. It was 4.30 a.m. I found an empty shower in which to dress, threw cold water on my face and we were ready to leave.

It was a cool, pleasant start to the day. In the dark, we crossed the medieval bridge over the Esla, which led us out onto the main N160. A mile further on, we crossed the main road and followed a hedged path running alongside the N120. We were confused by the map directions.

We met the young Dutch group, conferred together, re-crossed the road and took the track that ran alongside.

At Villamoros de Mansilla there was a bar. It was full of pilgrims eating breakfast. I ordered the usual toast, *marmelada* and *cafe con leche*. Stuart joined a Frenchman for a chat and I talked to a German group who passed my Swiss walking stick around for inspection, while Ann sat resting her foot on a chair.

2 km out of Villamoros, we came to a junction. We crossed the great twenty arch bridge, Puente de Villarente, over the Porma. Pilgrim guides of the twelfth-century mention this bridge, which has been restored and rebuilt many times over the years, due to flooding. After another gruelling walk by the roadside, we followed the yellow arrows to an inland track that evolved into a tedious, gradual climb uphill before descending into the suburbs of Leon. There were a few wildflowers on the sandy banks: harebells and daisies.

At Villarente, the little church had a stork's nest on its arch. In this part of Spain, most church towers had the obligatory stork's nest. No wonder there was so many children!

Stuart carried my rucksack for a while and walked with Ann, chatting away, while I dragged behind. The silicone inserts helped the soles of my feet, but because of the raised height, the upper part of my boots constantly rubbed and chafed. Ann limped, too. Her toe was now badly infected and her foot throbbed.

At the top of the hill by a walled graveyard sat Richard and Russ. We joined them for a rest and ate the yogurts we had bought yesterday. They raced ahead and we followed at a slower pace, admiring the panoramic view of the city of Leon.

Downhill to the main road, we were forced to follow the new motorway for 1 km. The pilgrim signs were swallowed up by the roadworks. We glimpsed a yellow arrow on the opposite side of the motorway. We dashed across the right-hand lane to the centre and struggled over the metal barriers. An amazing contortion with our rucksacks balanced on our shoulders. We saw some pilgrims walking along the motorway in the opposite direction. We yelled and screamed. They hurtled over and scrambled across the metal barriers in their turn.

We entered the Puente Castro district over the eighteenth-century bridge, which was quite impressive; a heron preened himself perched on the riverbank.

Embedded in the pavement were shell emblems in brass, which pointed in two directions. We argued about the route, our tempers short because of exhaustion and pain. We followed the shells that pointed to the old town area of Santa Ana. We hadn't any city maps and had no idea where we were going. The shells led us to a huge municipal hostel.

Richard and Russ were sitting outside when we arrived, waiting for the dormitories to open. Pilgrims rested on the stairs as they waited to register. We realized we had taken the wrong route and were teased by our friends when we confessed that we were staying at another Parador: the Hostal de San Marcos for two nights! We said goodbye, as we probably would not catch up with them again.

We headed toward the cathedral spire, assuming that the Plaza San Marcos would be close by. We were wrong.

By this time, Ann was unable to sit or stand. Her knee was swollen and her septic toe was throbbing. I ripped out my silicone soles and shuffled, cringing with every step. We asked the way and still got lost; worst of all, at a main junction Ann walked on, unable to focus through the pain.

Stuart helped me hobble along. We literally walked round in a circle. Eventually, a woman showed us the way through to the main *avenida* that led to the Plaza San Marcos. It was a long wide thoroughfare with a busy Sunday street market packed with people.

I didn't think I could go any further; Stuart and I sat on the steps of a building to rest. We saw Ann limping up the *avenida*, leaning on her trek stick as though it was a Zimmer frame. We were all furious at our stupidity in negotiating the city, but were rewarded by entering the huge plaza, full of fountains and neat box hedges.

A prominent feature was a fifteenth-century cross, relocated from the summit of the Portillo hill outside Leon. At the foot of the cross was a bronze statue of a suffering pilgrim gazing in anguish at the hostel. His bare toes protruded through rags wrapped around his feet, his broken sandals at his side. Nothing has changed in 500 years; exhaustion and pain are always part of the pilgrimage.

The Hostal San Marcos was originally a monastery and hostel built around 1515. It is now part of the Spanish chain of Paradors; a luxury hotel. As we checked in, the elegant guests gazed incredulously at our grubby, sweaty, sloppily dressed group.

There was no mail for me. I was very disappointed. I had hoped for another package.

We were to be joined here by Barbara from Washington, an old working colleague I had not seen for years. She was flying in to Leon from Lisbon where she had visited friends.

We arrived a day ahead and organized the rooms. It was wonderful to be in such luxury. I soaked in the bathtub, to the joy of my feet! I looked at the soles of my boots and could see they were cracked; one was almost in half. No wonder I was having trouble. I would have to buy new boots. I took photographs of the soles so that I could complain to the manufacturers when I got home.

We had a late lunch/dinner in the grand Parador restaurant. The meal was a delight. We relaxed and enjoyed a bottle of wine. It had been a gruelling day and it was wonderful to unwind. A delicious starter cocktail of fresh salmon, pineapple and cheese, followed by trout stuffed with wild mushrooms and ham. We pigged out on fruit salad with strawberries and cream for dessert! We didn't look at the bill; we decided we'd worry about it tomorrow. To hell with the cost!

The Parador encompassed a museum and its interior was filled with works of art. The courtyard was surrounded by magnificent statues set in arches, from which we could view the cloisters through the gardens. The monastery dates back to 1115 when Dona Sancha donated land near the bridge over the River Bernesga for a church and a hospital for the needy. In 1523, the chapter of the Order of St James of the Sword, with the backing of Ferdinand the Catholic, ordered the construction of the present-day building as its institution headquarters. The exterior decoration was splendid with scallop shells and crosses and a representation of St James over the entrance.

Leon originated as a Roman garrison whose purpose was to protect the mining area north of the peninsula. The city grew in size in the fourteenth-century, with the building of new defensive walls. The Italian pilgrim Domenico Laffi, from Bologna, Italy, wrote in his journal dated 1673:

76

There is a very large and well-endowed hospital facing the river, which is called Hostal San Marcos and which has a beautiful church, and there are some monks who give rations of food to pilgrims. And in the morning we went to Mass and they gave us alms for three months. We strolled around the city again, which is really beautiful, rich and spacious. There is a very big market which is full of all manner of merchandise…
(Lozano, 1999)

It was interesting to contemplate the cost of today's expensive meal at the Hostal San Marcos and the fact that I was walking to raise alms for the Wildlife Trust. The pilgrim's purpose in the twenty-first-century is somewhat different from that of Laffis in the sixteenth-century.

Monday 28th May
LEON

Enjoyed a late buffet breakfast. Delighted that my package had arrived: more teabags, underpants, T-shirt, vitamin pills and moisturizing cream! I patted myself on the back for my cleverness in organizing fresh supplies. Ann whined. She wanted a package containing new feet.

I faxed a report to the Wildlife Trust on my progress and sent my stained, dirty remnants to the Parador laundry. We had a day to relax in Leon. It was the tradition for pilgrims to rest a while in Leon before facing the Montes in the west and entering Galicia.

We were tempted to sightsee, but shopping was vital. Priority one: new boots! We headed down the *avenida* in search of a sports shop. Ann clutched her boot to take to the cobbler's for stretching. She walked along hip-hopping in one heavy boot and a light sandal; no one noticed. We passed a P*edicuro* – a chiropodist with a *farmacia* attached!

We fell in the door and begged the beautiful dark-haired Spanish nurse to repair our feet. She patched mine up and sold us new blister plasters. Ann was in a state. Her toe now looked badly infected. The nurse shook her head and refused to attend to it, directing Ann to the doctor next door, or the hospital.

Ann refused. 'They will tell me I should have it lanced and not walk on it for days and we can't afford to do that. I will do it myself tonight!' Which she did, sitting with her foot in a bidet of warm water, jabbing the toe with a needle until it drained!

We found a wonderful cobbler on the Plaza Calvo who said he would work on Ann's boot and we could pick it up later.

A large sports shop was nearby. Disgusted with the gigantic heavy sleeping bag that wallowed like an elephant in the bottom of her rucksack, Ann decided to buy a new lightweight one. This marvellous bag rolled up to the size of a loaf of bread.

I needed a new hat, as I'd lost my second one – and the zip on my bumbag wouldn't stay closed. Every time I bent over, my lipstick and face cream would drop on the floor and roll away. As these were essential items for any hiker, I looked for a new one without 'Present from Leon' or a designer logo printed on the front.

The boot decision was tough. I tried on every pair of boots my size in the store and none of them seemed comfortable, which was not surprising, due to the state of my feet. I finally chose a soft, fairly light suede pair.

Stuart agreed to take our unwanted items back to Brussels, and rushed off to the cash point to accommodate the mounting peseta cost as we piled our stuff on the counter.

I wore my new boots back to the hotel. They were torture, and the thought of walking hundreds of miles in them was horrifying. I wondered whether the cobbler could mend my old ones, maybe put on new soles. When Ann went to pick up her boot, I took mine along to see what they would say.

'Put 'em in the bin,' was the answer, 'no possible!'

It was very very hot and we returned to the Parador with our purchases, and sank into chairs in the bar for cold drinks and *bocadillos* for lunch.

Barbara arrived at 4.30 p.m. it was so good to see her land safely as planned. Stuart took an adjoining room and, despite our arrangements for senior rates for three beds, Stuart was given a double room for the price of a single. So I moved in with him to make more space for us all. We unpacked and repacked our rucksacks and passed over to Stuart all unwanted items. He had purchased a very large bag at the sports shop to carry everything! We related our adventures to Barbara and spent some time enjoying the Parador San Marcos and looking at its treasures.

The church had been beautifully restored; the carved roof was magnificent, with exquisite detail. The cloisters were filled with Roman tombstones found near Leon. The survivors' grief for their lost loved ones, particularly the children, was very clear. We had a strong sense of the pain and sorrow after almost 2,000 years. Some of the relics in the museum were bloodthirsty, glorying in death and destruction. One plaque represented a saint and his family; all of them, including the twelve children carried the swords of martyrdom. The motto of the Knights of Santiago, which originated in Leon, *'Rubet ensis sanguine Arabum'* (My sword is red with Arab blood), was particularly repellent. A carving of the burning of Jewish books by a Catholic interrogator caused us to realize that if grief had not changed over the centuries, neither had mindless persecution.

We planned to dine out that evening, but the restaurant we chose was a disappointment. Seated on a busy corner with lots of traffic, the food was poor but the company was good. We had plenty to talk about. After all, the main components of our pilgrimage were walking, eating, sleeping, eating, resting, eating, attending services, eating, and our appetites had become enormous.

We walked back to the San Marcos at dusk, across the square to the river bridge, the lamplight reflected on the water. We looked at the plaques between the pansy beds fronting the hotel. They represented the main towns and cities on the El Camino. This was a very special city for a hiatus from our pilgrimage and a perfect place to meet up with friends and family for the final stage.

Tuesday 29th May
LEON TO HOSPITAL DE ORBIGO

At another sumptuous buffet breakfast, we stuffed a few rolls in our pockets for lunch. It was decision time. We were to meet Ann's two sisters, Carolyn and Penny, and their friend Gwyneth at Leon bus depot around 3.30 p.m. Stuart was returning to Brussels via Madrid on the girls' incoming flight.

Initially, I had thought we would take the bus out of Leon to Astorga, but then realized we would miss the picturesque entrance into Astorga from the pilgrim way. Most of all, I did not want to skip the famous bridge on El Camino over the River Orbiga. We agreed we would head for Hospital de Orbigo. The refuge was favourably reviewed. It could accommodate thirty-six people and was situated on the riverbank. Would six of us get a space in the refuge, arriving late in the day? After a day's travel of two flights and two bus journeys, would the group appreciate a refuge with cold showers and unisex sleeping arrangements? We thought not and I picked at random a pension in Hospital de Orbigo and booked three twin-bedded rooms. I impressed myself as I made the reservation in my best Spanish on my mobile phone.

First port of call was the cobblers. I made the decision that my new boots could do with a stretch. He promised me they would be ready after siesta, around 3.30 p.m. We settled the Parador bill and left our rucksacks in their care while we went sightseeing.

The cathedral was at the top of our list. We took the *avenida*, the pilgrim path to the cathedral. The first cathedral was begun in 924 on land donated by Ordono II, on a site which had previously been Roman Baths.

The second, circa. 1084... had a hospice for the poor, sick, and pilgrims... The third cathedral, begun circa. 1175, was a showpiece, a magnificent large Romanesque structure meant to compete with other monumental churches of the pilgrimage road... the cathedral was completed in record time, largely because it had the solid financial backing of both the monarchy and the papacy... Contracts for carpenters, masons, and painters are still extant from the 1260s. To help recruit talented artisans, Alfonso X exempted a blacksmith, a glazier, and twenty sculptors from paying taxes... Leon's cathedral remains true to the spirit of thirteenth-century Gothic architecture... (We were advised to) watch the afternoon sun play on the sculpted portals and on the spires of the towers. When the sunlight strikes full on the rose window, go inside and stand for a few moments in the middle of the nave breathing in the colors of the light. Watch them change intensity as they glide across the floor while the sun drops. Think of how these soaring towers of stone, this vast open internal space, and these dancing colors must have blown the mind of your average medieval pilgrim. (Gitlitz and Davidson, 2000:248)

We enjoyed the tourist shops and looked at the books, purchased some souvenirs and sat in a plaza café to write cards and drink coffee. We met Stuart at the Plaza San Marcos and visited the museum adjoining the chapter house and cloister to marvel at the plaster carving with gold leaf and scallop shell decoration.

At noon we collected our rucksacks and took the tree-lined *avenida* flanking the river.

As we walked along together, a young woman stopped us. 'Please,' she said in broken English, 'my father, he is old and ill, but he would like to meet some pilgrims.'

The old man in a wheelchair huddled beneath a shawl on this sweltering hot day, shook our hands and smiled. '*Bon Camino*,' he murmured.

The young woman thanked us. 'Now he feels blessed,' she said.

But we felt blessed, too, as we realized the momentous effort we were making and the kindness and tolerance of the Spanish people toward the motley collection of pilgrims. We found a shady bench beneath chestnut and beech trees and ate our rolls.

Stuart had to get to the airport to check in for the Madrid flight. We crossed the *avenida* by the monument – los Reyes de Leon with its fountain. We stopped for an ice cream while Stuart hailed a cab. It was great to have him with us and I was sad to see him leave. He planned to telephone me on the mobile from the airport, to let us know when the girls arrived.

Ann and Barbara walked on to the bus depot and I rushed back to the cobbler; the boots were ready. I lost my bearings somehow, jumped into a taxi, and a few minutes later arrived at the depot. All the plazas and *avenidas* were beginning to look the same.

The bus depot was crowded and hot. The Hospital de Orbigo bus was due to leave at 5.30 p.m. Stuart rang to say the flight was delayed an hour. We bought cold drinks and waited. An hour later he called again: the flight hadn't landed yet. We were prepared to miss the bus, but there was a final call from Stuart on the Madrid plane: he had met everyone in the airport lounge and the girls were on their way by taxi. We rushed to the queue for tickets and waved them to the front of the line as they came through the door.

I was glad we had decided on Hospital de Orbigo. We arrived as the sun was going down. We passed the pilgrim refuge on the way to the hotel. The girls obtained their passports, and we studied a huge wall mural while we waited for them. It showed a part of the route ahead: high mountains, a stream flowing through an alpine meadow. It looked wonderful.

We wound our way through the town to the Puente de Orbigo; the Don Suero de Quinones Hostal was right on the river ridge. We could not have picked a more perfect place to start the last leg of our journey. We sat on the terrace marvelling at this old medieval bridge going back to 452. On two heavy piers, the bridge winds between hip-high parapets of rounded stone, which came from the river bed, 600 ft across, with a long succession of arches. In 900, it was the scene of a great clash with the Moors and Alfonso III The Great.

There is a romantic story attached to this bridge. In the early 1430s, a knight, Suero de Quinones, driven by his passion for a lady, wore an iron band around his neck to show that he was bound to her. She scorned his advances, sensible girl!

Full of bravado, Quinones then decided to hold a tourney. He challenged all knights to meet him on the Orbigo Bridge. The news spread throughout Europe and several bored young men took up the challenge. It reminds me of some of the flamboyant characters my daughter brought home! Suero had a life-sized dummy dressed like a herald pointing the way to the Orbigo bridge set up on the pilgrim road. July 11th, 1434, the tournament began. Suero and his nine companions vanquished all challengers from as far away as France, Italy, Germany and Portugal. At the close of the tournament on August 9th, Quinones then proclaimed to the crowds of fans in attendance that since he had defeated 300 knights, he now considered himself free of the lady. He removed the iron band and rode off to Compostela with his friends and presented a jewel-encrusted bangle as a symbol of his freedom from the prison of love. The bangle is still in the museum at Compostela, adorning some statue. I hope the young lady in question stayed quietly at home, listened to her parents, did her homework and ignored this testosterone jamboree. The town still honours Don Suero with a jousting festival between July 10th and August 9th each year.

Everyone walked the bridge and took photographs. We shopped at the local store for water and breakfast goodies.

The hotel had been extended and renovated over the years and was very comfortable. Its specialty was the local *trucha* –

trout. The walls of the little reception area were adorned with colourful murals and photographs of fishing competition winners holding up giant trout. Obviously a great fishing spot! The restaurant was charming and we ordered a splendid meal for our first evening. Trout soup for starters; it arrived with the head floating on top. I can't eat a meal when the eyeballs of the main dish are staring at me, but the Rioja wine was good and the beefsteaks delicious.

We were in fine spirits. Carolyn, who was a reflexologist, had massaged Ann's feet, so she had stopped whining for a while. Everyone was tired after the journey and this pleasant stopover was welcomed. There were other pilgrims at Don Suero that we had met before, a Dutch couple and two American boys. We exchanged news and wished each other *Bon Camino*.

Ann and I didn't want to rain on the parade, but we warned the neophyte backpackers of the hardships ahead; 'Don't expect this to be a luxury holiday,' we told them sternly.

Wednesday 30th May
Hospital de Orbigo to Astorga

We made a dawn start; everyone up at 6.00 a.m. Carolyn and Penny fussed and fumbled with their packs, unused to getting up before sunrise. Ann and I had learned to leave before dawn, to finish our walk before the heat of the day built up in the afternoon. If we arrived when the refuge opened, we usually had a choice of beds and a hot shower.

We aimed to reach Astorga by mid-morning. It was only 16 km, but uphill most of the way. We crossed a sandy bank and came out on the road. There were a few flowers on the track: poppies, daisies and mallows. The distant snow-capped mountains were closer now. We would begin ascending them tomorrow.

My newly stretched boots were giving my feet a hard time. I had not been on the road more than half an hour and I had to stow the boots in my rucksack and put on my sandals; no ankle support to help with the weight of the pack, but I soldiered on. Everyone was in good spirits, adjusting and manoeuvring rucksacks and gear. We each kept our own pace. Ann strode ahead followed by Penny and Barbara. I struggled at the end of the line.

The track was asphalt for a good part of the way until we began to climb up Monte de la Colomba, through holm oaks. We emerged onto a paved path with a track off into meadowland and hedgerows: just right for a picnic spot and the call of nature.

I had a good breakfast of yogurt, banana, orange juice and a madelaine.

We came to a village with a coffee bar, another welcome stop. The sun had risen and we peeled off and reorganized our rucksacks yet again. Through more holm oaks and scrub, onto a forest path which crossed an *arroya* – *arroyo grillo*; *grillo* means cricket. We could hear their cacophony as we crossed the valley and climbed up to a plateau and the peak of El Teleno. We could see Astorga, just visible in the distance. There was a choice of two paths into San Justo de la Vega; we chose the straightest. The fairytale turrets of Astorga loomed behind giant city walls. After crossing the railway line and walking over the triple arched Roman bridge, we entered the city by following the yellow arrows on the wall.

It was 11.00 a.m. and the municipal refuge did not open until 1.00 p.m. We decided to do some shopping before the stores closed for siesta. I found a well-stocked shoe shop with a collection of walking boots, including a good American brand. The proprietor sat me down and carefully chose the right size, persuading me to buy new socks and abandon the ones I was wearing. I was very pleased as they felt much more comfortable. He obviously cared about his customers, but I had spent more on boots than on food!

There was a long line of pilgrims waiting to check into the refuge at 1.00 p.m. The refuge was located in part of the local school. The children were laughing and shouting outside – no naps today.

The wardens were very particular about checking everyone individually and getting all our details. Ann, in true Florida style, looked very glamorous in her straw hat where poppies blazed, wearing shorts and showing a good pair of tanned legs. Regardless of the time, she made up her face every day, much to the amusement of other pilgrims.

'I don't care what people think,' she said, 'I am not going to have the uglies along with all my other ailments!'

I also made the effort but never looked as good!

After we had checked in, the senior warden took me aside and whispered, 'The American lady, your friend. She is sixty-seven years old?' He said he thought it could not be true. Ann looked far too young. She couldn't possibly be sixty-seven!

I assured him she wasn't lying. He gazed at her and followed us around! It made her day!

We were escorted upstairs to the dormitory; iron bunk beds crammed together, only a foot between them. It was hot, stuffy and very crowded.

There was a fight for space on the washing lines outside the windows. Ann and I were used to this, but the girls thought it very primitive. We assured them this was better than some places we had stayed. The showers were hot and had doors for privacy. Some refuges had no shower doors or curtains. We turned our backs, scrubbed off the dust of the road and ignored everyone. The beds were fairly clean and dry!

It was a free municipal hostel, subsidized by the El Camino organization in Santiago and supported by voluntary contributions from the pilgrims. We always paid what we thought the refuge was worth compared with local community contributions. After all, pilgrims spent money in their villages and towns.

We planned to pass the afternoon and evening enjoying the sights of Astorga and left our rucksacks in the dormitory. Before going out, I sat quietly in the corridor, examining my feet and renewing the plasters before putting on my new socks and sandals. One of the wardens came over, looked and shook his head; he pointed to a door with a red cross on it and insisted I visit the doctor who would be on duty at 6.00 p.m.

Astorga is the capital city of the Maragatos. Pilgrims entered the walls through the *Puerta del Sol* (The Sunshine Door), which still retains some Roman elements. It was an important Asturian enclave and gained prominence in Roman times as it was positioned at the junction between two of the most important Roman roads, the Via Traiana from Bordeaux and the Via de la Plata from Merida. This profoundly influenced its development and explains the entrepreneurial and commercial nature of the Maragatos.

Records show the existence of a bishop by 350. This area changed sides and religions during the following centuries, and many Maragatos, probably for survival, changed their religion accordingly.

> Some say they descend from (legendary) King Mauregato. Another etymology for their name is that because so many of them survived as carters and muleteers, unable to make a living from the rocky soil of these mountains, the Romans called them mercator, or merchants. Some believe they are an isolated group of Mozarabs who have preserved their customs. Others think them to be a remnant of Astures, Berbers, Visigoths, or even Carthaginians. Until the beginning of this century, the men's costume was wide breeches, white shirts, red garters, and slouch hats, while the women wore crescent hats, lacy mantles, heavy black skirts, and intricate filigree earrings that were noted by Arnold von Harff in the late fifteenth-century. (Gitlitz and Davidson, 2000:277)

It was a beautiful warm afternoon and we were overwhelmed with the sights around us. As we walked up the road leading to the cathedral, I took a picture of Gwyneth and Barbara. They looked minuscule against the towering spires, turrets and the great wall. We passed an enchanted ruined house with mullioned windows and carved doors. The garden was a jungle, beautiful and wild; bees and butterflies buzzed among the flowers and grass, and weeds surrounded an elegant stone fountain. We debated on its worth and what fun it would be to own the house and spend time renovating it and rescuing the secret garden. The road was named Judaica. Had this home been abandoned because of persecution?

We were becoming blasé about cathedrals, but this was something special. Its two great towers can be seen for miles. First built in the thirteenth-century, it has been restored many times. A figure on top of one of the tower pinnacles is of a Maragato hero, Pera Mato. The Renaissance high altar is a masterpiece by the Andalusian artist Gaspar Becerra, who was a pupil of Michelangelo and Raphael. Carvings encrusted in gold leaf glimmered in light cast by stained glass windows beneath an echoing domed roof. We stood in awe, waiting to see the priest to have our passports stamped. He was gossiping in whispers to another priest. Finally, we were shunted into a small enclave where, with great panache, he stamped our books. Barbara discovered the fee for lighting the altar was 100 pesetas. A magical sight indeed.

Almost next door is a cell in which prostitutes were imprisoned, to whom pilgrims would traditionally give part of their food

> ...as an act of charity. There is a cautionary inscription over the window: 'Consider how I have been judged, for your judgement will be the same; me yesterday, you today.' (Gitlitz and Davidson, 2000:274)

Were the johns pursued in those days, too?

Opposite the cathedral is Antonio Gaudi's neo-Gothic folly, the Bishop's Palace built between 1887–1893. Inside is a Museum of the Ways – dedicated to all the roads that lead to Astorga, with a special section on the pilgrim's way, with figures of St James dressed as a pilgrim. It was all very ornate and the décor totally over the top, but well worth a visit.

'A bit Disneyworldish,' Ann said, 'Mickey Mouse on speed!'

The plaza was flanked with silver birch. Leading off were little streets of attractive old houses. We stopped at a bakery café for tea and cake. Here I was introduced to *mantecadas*, a butter bun, unique to Astorga. Can't say it was anything special, but Eccles cakes and Chelsea buns aren't memorable either.

Siesta was over and the shops were open and we went our separate ways, planning to meet for supper. I took my old boots back to the shop where I had purchased the new ones and asked the owner to kindly mail them to me in the Isle of Man.

Carolyn and Ann insisted on coming with me as they wanted to see how I would convey the request in my limited Spanish. I put the boots in my new box and addressed it to myself and managed amazingly with my pidgin Spanish. I gave him 1,000 pesetas (about £4) for the postage, and 1,000 pesetas for himself. He was happy and Carolyn and Ann were bursting with glee at the silent movie gestures and contortions I made.

Back in the plaza, Ann and Carolyn bought cards and pilgrim shells for their rucksacks. The others had gone to an art shop we had seen that morning. By the time we found the shop, the girls had already left. I purchased a little pad and tiny box of paints. More weight, but so nice to have!

We were hungry, time to eat. Armed with my new paper, I stuck signs on strategically located poles to inform the stragglers that we were at 'The Apostle' restaurant by the plaza. We ordered soup of the day, which we understood to be minestrone. They served bottled vegetables, floating in a watery fluid and followed this with plain grilled trout. A disappointing meal.

We walked back towards the refuge and fell upon Barbara, Gwyneth and Penny sitting outside a café, finishing their dinner. We joined them for coffee. Their meal was half the price of ours and twice as good!

Back at the refuge, I debated whether to visit the pilgrims' *consultorio* (surgery) for foot treatment. Carolyn questioned their hygiene. I felt I would be safer tending to my own blisters; the cubicle looked dirty and untidy.

The hot, smelly dormitory was crowded. Some pilgrims opened windows to let in fresh air, others slammed them shut, muttering angrily about mosquitoes. Despite lights out, people came and went, pawing through their sacks and plastic bags for hours.

On my top bunk, I had a Chinese girl with an American boyfriend who cavorted happily all night! I was afraid their combined weight would collapse the bunk and crush me while I slept. A large, elderly Spanish pilgrim, whose snores I had encountered before en route, was in an adjoining bunk. Sadly, he kept me awake, but he had no trouble sleeping. I don't think he ever washed or changed his clothes!

Thursday 31st May
ASTORGA TO RABANAL DEL CAMINO

We struggled to get everyone up and out. A dawn argument prevailed as to which route we should take. We gave the yellow arrows a miss and followed other pilgrims on a short cut to the main NV1. After a kilometre walking on the main road dodging lorries as they hurtled by, yellow arrows directed us onto an asphalt track, which brought us to the village of Valdeviejas.

My feet were agony in the new boots. They felt as if they were on fire. Every step was excruciating. Oh, how I wished I had accepted the Astorga doctor's offer of care!

We stopped for an early breakfast picnic, shed our fleeces, donned sun tan lotion, and trudged on over the rough stone path. At Murias de Rechivaldo, a Maragato village, there was an old hermitage with yet another stork's nest on top. Stork families nested in every turret and tower from Puente de Orbigo onwards!

We stopped at the village store/café/trading post. Over coffee, the group persuaded me to take a taxi into Rabanal where I could surely find someone to tend to my feet. The little Maragato lady fussed around, whipping out biscuits and cakes in an effort to persuade us to buy breakfast. They looked delicious and we felt guilty, as we had already picnicked. She kindly telephoned for a taxi from Astorga and I reluctantly waved the group farewell and went ahead to Rabanal.

The road followed the Camino all the way. The girls trooped off in the crisp cold air, following the trail across the sierra. There were wild lavender bushes everywhere. Thatched Maragato cottages huddled together on the slopes and herds of sheep were being moved to high ground for the lush fresh grass of summer.

There was not a soul to be seen in Rabanal del Camino when I arrived at 8.00 a.m. Every house was bolted and shuttered. The taxi driver dropped me at the refuge, which was closed until 3.00 p.m. Rabanal was a small village. To my despair, there was no pharmacy or doctor. A bar was open and I had another coffee.

At the top of the village, a path led to a large field surrounded by tumbledown walls. I climbed through a gap and found a shady spot under trees to wile away the hours until everyone arrived. I took off my rucksack, spread my fleece on the ground and threw off my socks and boots. It was wonderful just sitting there in the peace and quiet. My feet cooled off. I felt quite elated to be alone and resting in this beautiful spot.

The view from the field was spectacular with the woods and hills and the distant glistening mountain tops. I remembered the paints I bought yesterday and did a little chalky picture, giving up some of my drinking water. My rucksack became a pillow and I dozed.

Suddenly awakened by a strange crawling sensation on my feet and legs, I leapt up and found myself covered in red ants. As fast as I whipped them off, they crawled back. My new boots were full of them. Thank God they didn't sting. They were long, skinny and moved fast. I hopped on one leg, pulling on my socks. It was an endless job to get rid of them. Did they enjoy old English mutton? Then I got cramp. I was beside myself!

At 11.30 a.m., pilgrims drifted into the village. One entered the field on the opposite side and waved, unaware that I was doubled up in agony. I finally pulled myself together, scrambled out of the field and down the hill. The track was full of wild lavender on the banks. I grabbed a handful; the smell was heavenly. Ann appeared round the corner, followed by the others.

The little restaurant in the village was now open and we piled in for lunch. They had a pilgrim's lunch menu of vegetable soup and lamb stew. In a warm rustic atmosphere, we ravenously enjoyed the steaming bowls of food.

After lunch, we joined the long queue outside the refuge, prepared to wait until 3.00 p.m. in order to get beds for the night. We took turns to wander off and take photos, while the others rested in orderly rows under the trees.

The Refugio Gaucelmo was formerly the parish priest's house. It was converted to a refuge by the Confraternity of St James in 1991. It is a typical L-shaped *maragato* house with patio, garden, barn and *huerta* (a vegetable garden and orchard).

We were in the converted barn with bunk beds and, ecstasy, an adjacent bathroom. This was the nicest refuge on the Camino. The wardens, all UK volunteers, made us very welcome. I was their first visitor from the Isle of Man.

The kitchen and dining area were spotless. We made cups of tea and took them out to the orchard meadow. One of the wardens brought us mattresses to lie on. This was the life! We spread out in the long fragrant grass under the fruit trees and enjoyed the afternoon. We did some washing and had a hot shower.

The senior warden gave me a big bowl of warm salt water to soak my feet. I punctured all the new blisters and put on skin plasters. I felt a lot happier. Another elderly English lady joined me. Her feet were bleeding and much worse than mine.

We explored the hamlet and found a little store at the bottom of the hill to purchase provisions for supper and picnic supplies for the next day. The locals were interested in us, and friendly. Most of the houses were very old, poorly maintained, with crumbling porticos and partly derelict.

Rabanal del Camino was at one time an important stop on the pilgrim's way, the last milestone before the final stage of the climb up Monte Irago. In the twelfth-century, the Knights Templar were garrisoned in the town. Their base in Rabanal would possibly have been a dependency or outpost of Ponferrada, with the function of ensuring safe passage on this difficult, lonely stretch up Monte Irago, or Mount Rabanal as it was sometimes called.

Some of the churches and pilgrim hospitals from this important era are still standing.

At 6.00 p.m. Barbara, Ann and I decided to go to vespers in the austere *refugio* chapel. Two monks chanted. They had beautiful voices. The little chapel was packed with pilgrims of all nationalities. Two enormous candles blazed beneath a plain carving of Christ on the cross above the altar. It was a moving, heartfelt service.

We enjoyed a supper of ham, tomatoes and crusty bread with a bottle of red wine. Carolyn and Gwyneth diced fresh fruit for salad.

I spent time before turning in looking at all the books and records in the Confraternity library. It was very interesting.

The warden approached me to settle a question his colleague had raised. 'Is the Isle of Man a separate country from the UK?' If so, could they have a flag for their map? They would then start a new page in the Confraternity book for pilgrims from the Isle of Man! They wanted details of The Manx Wildlife Trust, for whom I was walking. I assured them I would write and let them know how much I had raised and promised to send a flag, et cetera, as soon as I got back.

The warden joined us round the table in the kitchen to talk about the rest of the route. We had a week to get to Santiago. He suggested areas we could bus if we ran short of time and told us of the places we must see and the difficult ones we should avoid.

By the time we got into our bunks, the lights were out in the barn. An American guy on the top bunk behind me groaned in annoyance as I shuffled about trying to get my night gear on and organize my sleeping bag!

Friday 1st June
RABANAL DEL CAMINO TO
VILLAFRANCA DEL BIERZO

Up at 6.00 a.m. Breakfast already prepared for us in the refuge kitchen. We were waited on by the three wardens. Coffee, tea, toast and marmalade. All very British. One of the monks who had been chanting at vespers last night was in the courtyard. He looked quite different in old jeans and a Real Madrid T-shirt! Outside the refuge was a middle-aged man called John with a camper van. He had parked outside the refuge all night, which annoyed the wardens. From the UK, widowed, retired, and living on the Costa Blanca, he had driven the pilgrim trail and become fascinated with meeting pilgrims of all nationalities and enjoyed their company, or so he said. Portraying himself as a good Samaritan he offered lifts and help to pilgrims in distress.

The elderly English lady was in a bad way and took up his offer. She asked me if I would go with her? My feet felt so much better, but I knew the haul out of Rabanal was a tough one. I agreed to go 5 km just beyond Foncebadon, a ruined village.

We climbed out of Rabanal; it was so beautiful; fields of foxgloves and lilies in bloom. The walk up to Cruz de Fierro, the second highest point on the Camino, was breathtaking. It was 1.5 km above sea level.

> The enormous pile of stones at the summit may result from a variety of ancient customs. The pre-Roman Celts were in the habit of marking their high mountain passes with piles of rock (for which we still use the Gaelic word Cairns). Roman travellers also customarily marked high passes by leaving

stones, called murias, in honor of the god Mercury, the patron of travellers. The hermit Gaucelmo who topped the pile with a cross, essentially Christianized a pagan monument.

Many modern pilgrims who have picked up a large stone early in their journey as a symbol of the sins they hope to expunge by pilgrimage deposit them on the heights of Foncebadon as an act of contrition. (Gitlitz and Davidson, 2000:284)

The whole area was surrounded by miles of white and golden broom and mauve and white heather, a colourful patchwork with the snow-tipped mountains in the background. There was a chapel at the top, near the cairn of stones, built to memorialize the original hermitage and shelter built by Gaucelmo in the twelfth-century.

John was at the Hermitage making coffee for pilgrims as they arrived. It was a beautiful day with bright blue skies; cool and breezy on top of the pass and the coffee was welcome.

A scallop shell I had carried from home was now broken into two pieces. I added half the shell to the cairn and wrote boldly 'Isle of Man' on the stone above. Tucked in between the stones were hundreds of notes from pilgrims, money, coins, trinkets, boxes, ribbons and lots of heather. Messages were carved all over the pole. The girls arrived breathless and climbed in turns to the top of the stone mountain to take photographs. Finally we got a fellow pilgrim to snap all of us as we waved triumphantly from the top of the pile.

Today's route map covered 32 km to Ponferrada where there were numerous hostels and hotels. There was a basic refuge at Manjarin and another at Molinesca, which was about 20 km from the Cruz de Fierro. We tried not to be concerned about the huge distances we had to cover.

It was a pleasant path across the top from Cruz de Fierro. The colours and hues were striking and we marvelled at the view around us as we drank in the smell of gorse and broom and brushed through the tall heather. My feet were much better as my new canvas and leather boots were stretching and adapting to the shape of my feet. Cows grazed in a fertile meadow. They must have been brought up to these pastures from El Acebo. There was a copse of trees and a walled area where crosses stood at various angles, probably an old graveyard. We made a tortuous 2 km climb to the abandoned village of Manjarin, which had been a pilgrim hostel in the sixteenth-century. Manjarin now consisted of one or two shacks and a derelict barn.

These ramshackle buildings were run as a *refugio* by a bearded hippy character called Tomas who devoted his life, in a medieval manner, to the care of pilgrims in this high desolate spot where bad weather was the norm. Today however, we basked in brilliant sunshine and warmth. The *refugio* is not an official hostel and the electricity company cut off the supply when Tomas didn't pay his bill. He went to Leon and sat outside their office on hunger strike until they relented and reconnected him at no charge. Because of this publicity, he received a donation of twenty mattresses, a toilet and an outdoor kitchen. He had a little shop selling a few basics, along with cap and shell badges. His mileage signs on the roadside by the refuge were debatable but a colourful photo opportunity! They included Jerusalem 5,000 km, Machu Pichu 9,453 km, Rome 2,475 km and Santiago de Compostela 222 km.

Soon after Manjarin, at a summit in the road, just below a military radar station, we were at 1517 m – the highest point on the whole Camino. The view over the west face of Mont Irago was magnificent. We found a green and sheltered spot for a picnic and stretched out on the slope our legs dangling into space. We shared all the provisions we had left over from Rabanal. We were elated at the heights we had conquered. A Mont Irago high! I had never seen so much colour. I wanted to stay there forever and paint.

We descended through splendid open countryside to El Acebo. The village gave a glimpse of an almost vanished world. It was quiet and deserted but for two cows that wandered up the street to greet us. The ancient houses were still lived in. Balconies overhung the road with guttering that ran down the centre. Roses spewed off and around old walls, wrought iron gates and archways. It was a fascinating place.

We found a little bar and collapsed on the rickety chairs. There was a parrot in a cage on the wall, standing in his fresh water bowl, placidly snoozing.

Gwyneth looked at her burning, blistered feet and then at the parrot. 'Oh, how I wish I was that bird!' she exclaimed.

Our laughter woke up the parrot, which sidled away to the corner of his cage.

It was 3.30 p.m. and 8 km remained to Molinesca. We agreed we couldn't walk that distance. The girls were finished; they had walked 24 km. My feet had held out, but I knew that I couldn't manage much more. We had the suburbs of Ponferrada ahead of us and another 20 km to Villafranca. We asked the bar owner if he could ring Ponferrada for two taxis. He said he knew a man with one car who could make two trips! He arrived within twenty minutes in a big white car; he drove like a maniac. We reached Ponferrada very quickly.

The broom and heather gave way to banks of cistus and it was quite a scenic drive until we reached the city. He only charged us 2,000 pesetas, which is about £8. Everyone needed money and he took us to a bank that had a cash machine. It gave us an opportunity to view Ponferrada in comfort, a city in two distinct halves: the unspoilt and picturesque old quarter, and, across the river, the modern industrial area. Ponferrada first came to prominence in the eleventh-century as a result of the iron bridge over the Sil. We caught a glimpse of the impressive Templar Castle, which is said to be one of the finest examples of Spanish military architecture.

We whirled along the minor road that followed the Camino path into Villafranca. Beyond the industrial area, slag heaps and electrical power plant; we headed out across fertile farmland and vineyards. The driver took us to a private refuge, Ave Fenix, which was situated at the top of the town, next to the Church of Santiago. The Spanish Pope Calixto III (1455–

1458) granted a concession to pilgrims unable to continue their journey, allowing them to stop at this church and receive the absolution and plenary indulgence they would have received reaching the apostle's tomb in Compostela.

We became hysterical with laughter when Carolyn stepped out of the taxi and the driver hauled her rucksack from the boot. A transparent plastic water tube on the top of her pack came loose and flopped on the ground at the driver's feet. He jumped back in horror, under the impression he had broken some kind of life support system. He gazed at Carolyn in admiration. What a heroic pilgrim lady to walk under such handicapped conditions!

The refuge was rustic and ramshackle. We looked at the main dormitory with a few beds left and noticed a separate door to a smaller dorm with a sign on it saying '*Reservado* 40 *anos*' (reserved for 40 years+) – that was us! Fifty and sixty *anos*, if the truth be told.

There were a few bunks left; I took a top one. The roof was thatched and the beams were dust covered. Thick spider webs hung down. There was plenty of wildlife in the roof! There had been a fire here and the family had elaborate plans to build a new hostel. The Jesus Jata family ran the hostel and, according to the guide, devoted their lives to looking after pilgrims. We found them sullen, tired and irritable. Perhaps the constant crowd of ungrateful pilgrims had soured them over the years.

The place was run down and dirty. The shower block, toilets and wash basins were in the outside courtyard. There was little privacy. The guide indicated they served a full meal with wine. The dining area adjoined the squalid kitchen. There was a counter in the dining area where tourist brochures, tacky souvenirs and dusty snacks were displayed. We decided on tea and coffee and some madelaines to revive us until dinner. We complained about the lukewarm drinks when, to our horror, we saw the daughter fill the cups from the hot tap.

We decided to explore the town and find a restaurant.

Barbara was anxious to discuss the route and our plans. She was concerned that we would not make Santiago by the 7th at the rate we were going. Ann and I poured over the maps and tried to make a decision. Barbara was keen to miss out O Cebreiro because of the long climb. If we took the planned route up to Sarria by way of Samos we would then have another day to descend and we couldn't possibly get through Galicia in the three days we had left. I needed to think quietly about our dilemma. I went for a walk in the garden – if you could call it that – which consisted of a moth-eaten vegetable patch and a few fruit trees.

I had so wanted to do O Cebreiro, but I could see there was a problem. I wished we had not booked our return flights; two or three extra days would have given us the time we needed. When the son of Jesus Jato said to me they could arrange for our rucksacks to be taken up to O Cebreiro, I was tempted to persuade everyone to leave out a piece of Galicia instead. But to obtain a pilgrim certificate in Santiago our passports needed to be stamped to show we had walked the last 100km.

Ann and Penny talked of hiring another taxi. The refuge did not like us talking about cars and taxis but, under duress, gave us three numbers to ring. We did not have the true pilgrim spirit!

Villafranca del Bierzo was an interesting old town. We stopped arguing and went off to explore. The Castle of the Marquesses of Villafranca with great old walls lay just below us and the path into town was lined with historical monuments. The sixteenth-century castle is now owned by the Alvarez de Toledo family and is the favourite haunt of the composer Chistopher Halffter.

Barbara, Gwyneth, Carolyn and I wandered down to the river bridge, where there was a contemporary statue of a pilgrim carrying a gourd water bottle tied to his staff. It was a lovely town with views to the hills. We met up with Ann and

Penny in the square for a meal at a little café. We sat outside and continued to mull over our plans. If we left at the crack of dawn, it would be too dark to attempt the path to O Cebreiro. If we left at first light we wouldn't see anything anyway because of the thick mists. I could see I was being talked out of O Cebreiro!

The café food was poor, the salad limp and the chips soggy; I was beginning to feel depressed about everything. My stomach began to rebel! We found the supermarket for some wholesome picnic shopping.

Barbara came to me clutching two kitchen sponges. 'Would they be good for shoulder rucksack supports?' We thought it was a brilliant idea and cleared the shelves. We piled the sponges up on the counter; pink, blue and lemon ones. The checkout *chica* was bemused.

We walked back to the refuge at dusk, and took a narrow path under the trees below the castle. We listened to a nightingale singing in a tree above us.

We arrived back too late to book a taxi and decided to try and follow the confusing bus timetables. It was dark now; all we had was a fading torch, but we needed to plan our next move. Carolyn was disturbed because she had seen rats. We decided to turn in and make final plans early in the morning. It had been a long day and we were exhausted.

Saturday 2nd June
VILLAFRANCA DEL BIERZO TO
SARRIA AND PORTOMARIN

A very disturbed night. I woke at 3.30 a.m., convinced I saw everyone getting dressed and walking out of the door! I slid down off my bunk in a daze, grabbed my rucksack, boots and clothes, dropped them several times and thundered out of the door, which slammed back against the wall. I bolted through the courtyard, washed, brushed my teeth and began to dress when I realized no one else was there.

I sat on the bench in the yard and hunted for my watch. I was stunned to find it was only 3.40 a.m. My sleeping bag was still spread out on the bunk. As I crept back inside, the door crashed closed again. In the dark I reached for the upper bunk ladder, it fell to the floor, narrowly missing the outstretched arm of the portly middle-aged Brazilian sleeper below. She woke with a groan. By now everyone else was stirring, moaning and groaning. Torches flashed as people checked the time! I lay silently on my bunk, afraid to move a muscle and finally fell back to sleep. At 6.30 a.m., I was the last one up!

The plan was to catch the 8.15 a.m. bus on the other side of town by the main NV1. We had a poor refuge breakfast of stale bread and jam and lukewarm coffee. Jesus Jato senior tried to explain in Spanish the location of the bus stop. I was unsure, the route sounded so complicated. He directed me to his old car. He would show me the way. The rust bucket had a hole in the floor and it took him a while to get the thing started. We shot off, exhaust roaring and went perilously downhill in a cloud of smoke. I had my notebook and pen ready to make notes of landmarks; I didn't want to miss anything. The car, shuddering away, crawled back uphill to the refuge.

The girls were ready and waiting. It was a lovely morning, fresh, bright and sunny, but we could see the thick clouds of mist swirling around the hills to O Cebreiro. I led everyone through the town and onto the N1V; we waited in a lay-by for the bus.

It was almost 8.15 a.m. when, to our surprise, John came rolling around the corner in his camper van. He pulled in sharply and told us he was moving up the Camino. He enquired where we wanted to go?

We suggested Sarria as it was within walking distance of Portomarin. We crammed in and he asked Penny to sit in front with him to read the map. We cheerfully sacrificed her, sniggered like teenagers, and lolled on the cushions in the back to rest our aching bones.

Along the N1V, we climbed high through wooded countryside and rolling mists. We stopped on a high plain for a breakfast picnic. It was quite eerie looking down on the thick banks of cloud. John set out his table and chairs and served hot strong coffee. It was a nerve-racking haul up into Sarria. Manoeuvering the old camper van through the narrow streets of the antiquated town was a nightmare.

We insisted on giving 10,000 pesetas to John for his time and trouble. It had been well worth it. I knew then that it was impossible for us to have walked the distance in less than two days. We parked outside the Church of Santa Marina at the top of the town. The side of the hill was crowned by the castle. We were on the Calle Mayor, the pilgrim route.

On the church door was a notice, which stated that pilgrims must register with the Guardia Civil across the street. This was novel; we hadn't been asked to do that before. All very official, the guards perused our passports and stamped them one by one with a great flourish. We were questioned as to our point of origin on the Camino and our final destination. It then occurred to me that the pilgrim route could be great cover for more sinister reasons. We were eager to get walking as we had many miles to cover.

We were now in the province of Lugo, in Galicia. We followed the pilgrim route steeply downhill past the monastery of La Magdalena. We stopped to have our picnic by the Roman bridge, Ponte Aspera, which crossed the Celeiro river. Farmers were busy cutting the hay and a tractor shunted the bales back and forth over the bridge. We were at the little village of Sancti Michaelis in which a stone marker indicated 105 km to Santiago! What a change from the 760 km with which we started. We walked uphill to Vilei through a beautiful wood of chestnuts and ancient, gnarled oaks.

Finally we emerged on an asphalt track leading to the church of Santiago de Barbadelo dating back to the ninth-century. The main portal was adorned with a crude figure with outstretched arms. Animals drank from a vessel beside this Christ-like figure. There were carvings of roses on the side of the door.

As we walked up the track from Barbadelo, there was a wooded copse with plastic seats set enticingly under the trees. An enterprising Spaniard sold cold drinks and ice cream from a little van. He had authority to stamp our passports. Civil guard to ice cream vendor; it seemed anyone could become a passport stamper on the pilgrim route.

Ann was feeling very tired; her knee had swollen to the size of a grapefruit and she was permanently wearing the knee brace she had purchased in Leon. Resting her leg on a chair, she fell asleep immediately, ice cream dripping down her chin. Refreshed and sticky with ice cream, we moved on.

This was a day of changing scenery. The route was dotted with farming hamlets, sleek, fat cows and gurgling streams. There was a Celtic inheritance here with slate stone walls and vaulted leaning stones encircling gnarled dead trees. Banks of tall foxgloves flanked the paths and golden clumps of broom shimmered in the sunlight. We climbed up a riverbed; the stream ran downhill around us, gurgled and splashed over our boots as we jumped from stone to stone. Translucent blue/green dragonflies hovered over the water. Farmers were busy with haymaking. Medieval grain stores or corn cribs, *hórreo* in Spanish, were still being used to store the harvest. With ornate crosses on the top they looked like mini chapels.

We reached the sleepy village of Morgade, at the foot of Monte Morgade. There was a house with a slate board propped outside the door. Chalked on it was a menu for pilgrims. Through the beaded doorway, sheltered from the sun, doing their homework at the table was a girl of about fourteen, with her younger sister. The lunch menu was over but they could bring us vegetable soup and omelettes. We were impressed with these industrious girls; they set the table outside and served us fresh water and warm rolls. The soup was potatoes and greens; never had such a horrible-looking mixture tasted so delicious!

We knew we would not make Portomarin as it was 4.00 p.m. We decided to walk to the hostel at Ferreiros. The countryside was rugged with a steep climb to the village. The friendly hostel had twenty-two beds, but they were filled. It was early evening and we were exhausted. The warden offered to ring for transportation into Portomarin.

Carolyn felt we should go to a hotel or pension; we needed a hot shower and a decent bed. I dug out my mobile, picked one of the hotels mentioned in the guide, and booked three double rooms for the night. Everyone was ecstatic.

Meson de Rodriquez welcomed us to its freshly painted, enlarged pension. We had a superb view over the dam. Portomarin is a new town, built when the old one was 'drowned' by the waters of the Belesar dam. The medieval bridge was submerged along with the rest of the town, which had records dating back to 993. A pillar of the medieval bridge was saved for posterity and erected at the mouth of the new bridge.

The church of San Nicholas had been the headquarters of St John of Jerusalem and was preserved. The church was dismantled stone by stone in 1956 and rebuilt in its present town centre position, close by the Meson de Rodriquez. In 1962, the new Portomarin was inaugurated higher up the bank.

It was very odd to be in this modern town with streamlined apartments and houses, well-stocked shops and a glistening supermarket. The streets were wide boulevards designed in a grid-like pattern. We had walked through a medieval world all day long, transported back in time. Families made hay with wide wooden rakes on the hillsides; a farmer scythed his hay while his oxen, still yoked in their hames, munched the lush green grass and the cart was drawn up by the side of the lane. Small cottages clustered together on muddy cobbled streets. Modern farm equipment was used alongside ancient hand-made wooden implements. It was unbelievable; we had walked from this into modern Portomarin within the space of a few minutes, from one time warp to another.

We were too tired to explore; we enjoyed hot showers and sank into soft beds with fresh clean-smelling linen. We could hear the distant purr of a nightjar as he sang by the dam banks.

Gwnyth and Barbara, Astorga

Top: Rucksack reorg, Carolyn and Barbara
Bottom: Local interest, Rabanal

Waiting for the refuge to open, Rabanal

Top of the 'pile', Cruz de Fierro

Top: Isle of Man shell joins the 'pile', Cruz de Fierro
Bottom: Stone wall resting spot en route El Acebo

Top: Marching into El Acebo
Bottom: Barbara, Gwynyth and Carolyn, the pilgrim statue, Villafranca

Top: A tired Ann, Barbadelo
Bottom: Vito from Canada meets the locals, Gonzar

Top: En route Palais de Rei
Bottom: Sponge shoulder pads and pockets filled with seeds
and raisons

Top: Basking in the sun, Melide
Bottom: 'A queimadas' – Brazilian master of ceremonies,
Melide

Top: Breakfast with John en route to Sarria
Bottom: Farmyard followers, Raido

The 'Galician Cheese Maid', Arzua

The Statue of St. James, Boente de Baixo

The 69 Km milestone to Santiago

A dog joined us on the misty walk from Arzua

Top: Santiago at last
Bottom: The brass band and the *nino*, Santiago

Top: Barbara departs Santiago
Bottom: Proof of journey – receiving the certificate, Santiago

Sunday 3rd June
PORTOMARIN TO PALAIS DE REI

We were ready to leave at 6.00 a.m. when I remembered that the receptionist had kept my passport when we registered. It was pitch black; I turned on the reception area lights. Nobody was about. I climbed over the counter and looked in the cubbyhole displaying our room number. The passport wasn't there!

The pension café was due to open at 7.00 a.m. and we were forced to wait until the owner arrived. He had left my passport in the café because he thought we would be having breakfast there. When the girls heard breakfast was included in the price of the room they rushed to a table to enjoy steaming *café con leche* and *tostada*!

We had planned to walk 25 km, but with all the distractions we made a late start. The pilgrim way led through the quiet town, down to the dam and across a narrow footbridge. The huge lake was calm and beautiful in the early morning mist. We had a gentle climb round the north side of Monte San Antonio through woodland.

There was a Camino milestone at San Mamed; only 69 km left to Santiago. Moisture dripped from the trees and I had never seen so many cobwebs trembling with dewdrops. They made a magical scene around us. At one point there was a high bank where trees met across the path. It was like walking through a tunnel. We splashed along riverbeds clumped with slate and stones. Slabs of granite bridged streams alive with tadpoles and frogs. At the hamlet of Gonzar we walked by the road for a few kilometres. Through the mist we saw a strange figure hauling a cart. It was Vito from Canada. He had flown into Leon with his golf cart converted to carry a suitcase. His mascot, Wilson, a teddy bear wearing flying goggles, was attached to the front! The cart's wheels had punctured, and in-flight repairs had been performed using black electrical tape. He dragged his lopsided wobbling cart along the road. A farmer shouldering a scythe on his way to the fields came to look; he chuckled and shook his head! We didn't see Vito again, but I felt he would have had to abandon his golf cart!

It was very rural, the farming hamlets were quite primitive. A stout old woman washed clothes in a stone trough through which flowed water diverted from a stream. This was obviously the village laundromat.

Hay was lying in swathes in the meadows, families worked together in the fields, raking and tossing the hay into horse-drawn carts. We walked through cowpats with dairy smells everywhere. Cows mooed, chickens, chicks and ducks clucked, geese cackled and dogs barked. Plenty of lively farmyard activity. The farmhouses were ramshackle and rundown. The roadside banks were filled with small white marguerites. We passed a meadow full of golden daisies. There were foxgloves, gentian, dog roses, wild lupins, broom and heather as we got higher.

We stopped on the roadside for coffee and ice cream at a smart little garden café. Here we met Frederick and his wife with their blind dog, Digu, carried in a chest pouch like a baby. They had flown to Leon from Brazil via Madrid and planned to walk all the way to Santiago, staying at hotels as the refuges would not take pets. We photographed each other on the garden steps.

At Ligonde, in a converted Galician house, was a bar run by an evangelical group. We stopped for a chat. The church has a Roman portal and belonged to the order of St James. There are the remains of a pilgrim cemetery outside the village, which was formerly an important stop on the pilgrim route.

Once the mist cleared, it was very hot. By midday we were flagging and found it hard to keep up a good pace. Penny had blistered feet and collapsed in a field off the path. She needed to rest and insisted we go on and she would catch up later.

We walked for a mile and came to a junction of the Camino and the main road. There was a smart rustic restaurant serving Sunday lunches. Exactly what we needed. Ann and Carolyn opted to go back and find Penny as they were convinced she would be raped or murdered, if she was sleeping in an isolated field miles from anywhere. All they got for their pains was a wild-haired, disgruntled human being who fussed and muttered about bullying older sisters all the way back to the restaurant. It was 3.30 p.m. and the place was buzzing. We had a very enjoyable lunch of grilled sole and salad.

Our final 3 km into Palais de Rei (Royal Palace) followed the road. The town seemed dull and depressing. We hardly saw anyone on the streets; shuttered houses and closed shops lined the route. We expected to see a palace, but there was none in sight. There was a royal palace in the ninth-century, of which nothing remains. The only sign of a medieval past was a building, decorated with scallop shells, which was said to have been a pilgrim hospice. An interesting snippet translated from Latin in the pilgrim records of Aymeric Picaud in 1130:

> Innkeepers' servants along the road to Santiago who, taking pleasure in seduction for illicit gain, are inspired by the Devil himself to get into pilgrims' beds at night, are fully reprehensible. Harlots who go out to meet pilgrims in wild parts between Portomarin and Palais de Rei for this purpose should not only be excommunicated, but also stripped of everything and exposed to public ridicule, after having their noses cut off... (Lozano, 1999)

This sounds like an extreme reaction toward working girls! Why did he take the moral high ground? Obviously attracted to these harlots, he wished to destroy their appearance by cutting off their noses. Was he robbed, cheated or ignored?

There was a hostel sign at a bar and we asked about rooms for the night. The owner said the hostel was full but she had keys for another place. We followed her along the road to a new four-storey apartment building. We were the first visitors; everything was new. In fact, it wasn't really completed. There were no lampshades or bedside lights; it was very basic but the bathrooms were spanking new with hot water and the beds comfortable. It was reasonable at 2,400 pesetas each for the night (not quite £10).

The town was uninteresting. We found a café/bar where we managed to get some weak tea and a few nibbles. We passed a fruit shop on our way back to the pension and stocked up for the next day. The rest of the evening was spent attending to blisters, washing out socks and underwear. Barbara and I strung up a line and christened the new bathroom. We had covered the requisite 25 km that day and were totally exhausted.

Monday 4th June
PALAIS DE REI TO MELIDE

We left Palais de Rei at 7.00 a.m. On the Camino route out of town we stopped at a bar for breakfast. Two men were loading rucksacks into a rusty German tour bus. The tour group had parked the bus in a side street. Last night bogus pilgrims would have put on their packs and trotted off to register in the refuge. It was not surprising that the refuges were always filled, this represented a cheap holiday for people 'in the know'. I felt Picaud's words applied here: 'Excommunicate them and cut off their noses.'

Palais de Rei had placed a modern pilgrim statue on the Camino outside town. Even small towns valued and supported the pilgrims. We headed for Melide, 20 km away.

The route was studded with tiny farming hamlets. The morning chorus of farm animals greeted us as we strode along, fording streams and splashing by muddy wetlands. We passed a thriving picturesque area of bulrushes and yellow iris, and marshes full of croaking bullfrogs. We walked through dense vegetation to Outeiro da Ponte and crossed the River Pambre to the hamlet of Pontecampaña; then climbed up through a wood of oak and pine. There were pinky mauve miniature wild iris, mingled with gorse and broom on top of the hill. There was much to feast our eyes on. We saw hand crafted wooden farm wagons, standing derelict next to moss-covered rusted farm implements. At Leboreiro clustered beside the ancient roadway were stone cottages smothered with roses and grapevines, which seemed to be the only things holding their slanting walls and sagging roofs together. One tumbledown grey building, founded as a hospice by the Ulloa family in the twelfth-century, still had their coat of arms carved on the lintel.

At Furelos, named after the adjacent river, we crossed the magnificent medieval bridge – Ponte Velha with its four wide arches. We stopped in the town for a cold orange drink and I raided my pockets for some raisins and sunflower seeds. I needed them for strength to keep me going.

We met an English girl, Ruth, who had been in a recent much-publicized Valencia coach crash. She showed us her damaged jacket covered with burn holes from sparks generated by the accident. She was recovering from a broken arm, glad to be alive, and hoped the walk would help her become reconciled to the tragedy. Like our companions, she had joined the Camino at Leon.

Melide was a busy market town. We entered through the San Pedro district: not very inspiring. The refuge was part of a large municipal building next to the post office. It had 130 beds, stables and a washing machine, which we fell upon with joy. We washed our clothes, used all the line space then spread the rest on the warm stone wall. I nodded off as I rested in the sunshine, listening to the bees humming in the blossoms.

Later in the afternoon, we left to explore the old town. It was ramshackle, but interesting. The church of Santa Maria de Melide had an elaborate altar enveloped in beautifully arranged white flowers. There were amazing bloodthirsty frescoes depicting St James as 'the Moor-Slayer'. The priest stamped our passports. A peaceful square, surrounded by tall, shuttered houses, had a charming fountain crowned with a renaissance image of the Madonna and child, a flower box of petunias at her feet. On the way back to the hostel we enjoyed delicious pizza at an Italian restaurant. It was so nice and reasonable that we decided to return for our evening meal.

We showered, packed away our clean laundry and napped before going out to eat. We bought supplies at the local store, and succulent fruit at the greengrocers. After two bottles of wine with dinner we were in high spirits. The Italian food was a change. I couldn't manage to eat my huge portion of lasagne. We felt we had let the Spanish down. *Pulpo* (octopus) is the Galician delicacy and on all the menus, but so far we hadn't had the courage to sample any!

Back at the *refugio* we found a lively gathering in the kitchen preparing for a *queimadas*; a burning ceremony. A Brazilian group were mixing an alcoholic concoction, which they set alight! A tall handsome guy stirred the potion with a wooden spoon and chanted spells, supposedly to raise the spirits and ward off evil. We didn't understand a word. I took a drink from the fiery pot; my throat burned. The fumes wafted through to the dormitory and sleepy pilgrims got up to join the party. The master of ceremonies kept chanting until the wooden spoon caught fire. I found the drink very powerful after the wine and fell asleep the moment my head hit the pillow.

Tuesday 5th June
MELIDE TO ARZUA

We passed a seedy bar on our way out of town, with the usual rubbish-covered floor of cigarette ends and food wrappers. Already hardened locals were propping up the bar, puffing away, knocking back brandies and coffee. Steaming *café con leche* arrived in glasses, impossible to pick up without scalding our hands. I left the glass on the table and bent down to drink. I scorched my nose! A sock as a glove was the best bet – and a great way to air out last night's washing!

We rushed through our coffee breakfast. We had made an early start and wanted to be well on our way before sun up.

We followed the main road and crossed the River Lazaro. An asphalt path led us to a leafy oak and eucalyptus wood. The fragrant smell of the eucalyptus in the damp, misty early morning air filled us with energy. There were mature trees and plantations of saplings. A large golden dog, an Alsatian cross, appeared from nowhere and joined the group. He strolled through the woods with us, pink tongue lolling, and disappeared when we came onto the road again. Another friendly Spaniard!

Our first village was Raido. We halted abruptly on the muddy track and a group of Dutch bikers who had followed the road were also forced to stop. A herd of cows were being driven to new pasture. They rubbed against each other as they clattered by, beautiful beasts with sleek, velvety coats. The farmer's wife waved her stick and wished us all '*Bon Camino!*'

Red roses climbed abundantly over the fence by their old farmhouse and a great patch of marguerite daisies flooded through the gate. We soon left the road on a dirt track that led us through pines and ferns. After crossing a stream we arrived at the village of Peroxa. On the outskirts of the village we went through a tunnel that was perilous as the odd car whizzed through. We worked our way downhill to Boente. There were pretty hedgerows of escallonia (pinky flower) that reminded me of my Laxey Glen back home in the Isle of Man.

First came Boente de Riba followed by Boente de Baixo. Boente must have been an important halt on the Galician stretch of the Pilgrims Way at one time, as it is mentioned in Picaud's guide of 1130 and has a church dedicated to St James.

As we crossed the road at Baixo, a priest stood outside his church waiting to greet us. He ushered us inside to be blessed. We were spellbound by the beauty of this little place. The statue above the altar was of St James, wrapped in a rich red cape, seated on a throne. The altar had an embossed golden scallop shell and sword emblem dated 1846. The building was old but the interior fairly new in Camino years! The priest was shrewd; there was a secondary gain to his blessing. He directed us to the donation box as we left!

We stopped to rest and picnic by a stream. We were all suffering with blisters.

Onward through desolate hamlets and a further climb through eucalyptus. The sweet perfume of a hedgerow of double dog roses added to the pleasurable scents of the day. At the top of the hill we saw the road cut across the pilgrim's route. Our path descended a deep gorge only negotiable by some hazardously steep and flimsy wooden steps. Once we reached the other side, the path dropped quickly to the River Iso and we came to Ribadiso de Baixo. There was a delightful refuge here by the river. We stopped to look around. For once the guidebook gave a true account of the building: '…a beautifully restored magnificent refuge that offers all necessary facilities.'

We discussed staying here rather than going onto Arzua, but we were out of food and would have to go to Arzua for supplies anyway. We took time out to enjoy the surroundings.

Penny dozed off on the riverbank while we lazed on the grass, listening to the river gurgling along. Reluctantly we moved on and after Ribadiso de Riba we went through our second tunnel of the day and followed the path to the market town of Arzua, reknowed for its cheese.

The municipal refuge was the Old Music School, converted to a hostel with fifty beds. It had a spanking new kitchen, but no pots, pans or crockery! The dining room led onto a large patio, festooned with washing lines. We did the usual laundry, showering and chores before food shopping.

The old town had a charming square with lovely trees, two statues placed at either end. One was of a Galician cheese maker, a smiling young girl, with cheeses at her feet. It reminded us of a line from the film *The Life of Brian*: 'Blessed are the cheese makers'. The other statue commemorated the children of these rural communities who assisted their families by caring for the milk calves.

Pulpo (octopus) was still the main dish here, served spiced on wooden platters with hunks of bread washed down with the Ribeiro wine of the region.

We were all tired. The *pulporias* (octopus restaurants) did not open until 8.00 p.m., so we opted to buy a selection of cheese, tomatoes, plums, peppers and onions for dinner at the refuge. We carried one of the dining room tables outside onto the patio and were enjoying our repast with a bottle of wine when Richard and Russ arrived. They looked very tired and worn, and had walked every inch of the way. Richard had taken 100 films that he had mailed on to his publisher in Germany. He was pleased with all his material as he was going to produce a photographic journal of the Camino. He planned to donate the proceeds from the publication to the African Aids Mission.

The old Music School was a peaceful hostel. The dormitory balcony overlooked the street. We had an early night in anticipation of tomorrow. There were only two long walking days ahead of us, then Santiago at last.

Wednesday 6th June
ARZUA TO SANTIAGO

Arzua to Santiago was 39 km. We decided to go as far as Arca which would leave us 18 km to cover on Thursday, hopefully allowing enough time for us to attend the Pilgrim Mass at noon in the cathedral.

We left Arzua at 6.30 a.m., walking through the quiet town by scores of small vegetable patches which reminded me of allotments in World War II. After a short while, we came out onto the N547 and crossed the road back onto a farm track. We walked through hamlet after hamlet. There were lots of lovely wooded walks between the villages. We stopped for a picnic breakfast amongst tall ferns and shady trees, sitting on stacked stone slabs that had been used to build the bridge over a nearby stream. It was cool and tranquil, with nothing but birdsong to be heard. Shafts of sunlight pierced through the leafy trees and cast patterns on the grass.

We took a bathroom break, crouching among the ferns. I looked back at everyone, their heads bobbing as they zipped and unzipped. They looked like children playing hide and seek. I couldn't resist. I shouted, 'Ready or not, here I come!'

We arrived at a village where an enterprising elderly Galician couple had rearranged their garden as a café selling fruit and drinks. We had coffee in a variety of battered mugs and sat down on benches in the sunshine. Frederico from Brazil arrived with his wife and little dog Digu and we took more photographs. Crowing cockerels, a peahen and barking dogs agitated the blind Digu and they were soon on their way. The owners took our mugs and washed them with a garden hose in an old stone sink. I doubt whether this pilgrim café would meet with EEC health regulations!

After Salceda there was a meadow full of orchids. I snapped a splendid picture of a burnet moth poised on a blossom. Another eucalyptus forest (the wood is used by the Spanish for furniture and paper) brought us to hamlets with magical names: Ras, Xen, Brea, Empalme and Santa Irene, where there was a little chapel dedicated to the Portuguese Martyr, Saint Irene,

> …with Agape and Chione, martyr during Diocletian persecution. Even after her companions were burned, Irene steadfastly refused to eat Roman sacrificial food. She was cast naked into the soldiers' brothel, but no one dared touch her. Eventually, she, too, was burned. Apr. 3. (Gitlitz and Davidson, 2000:399)

There were delightful scenes of sleepy fat cows lying under shady trees and the smell of freshly mowed hay permeated the air. Old ruined buildings were covered with vines and pennywort. Ancient family crests carved deeply into the stone remained intact next to crumbling window frames. We walked back in time in Galicia. There was a memorial to a pilgrim, named Guillermo Watt who died between these hamlets in 1993. His family wished him to be remembered by the pilgrims who walked the Camino path. They had his hiking boots cast in bronze and set into a niche in the wall. We stopped to offer a prayer, then wound some wild flowers around the burnished shoes.

Back on the N547, we were unhappy to see the roadside verges were being sprayed with weedkiller. I hoped it was herbicidal, but it was doubtful. We passed a sawmill then downhill through the villages of Rua and Burgo and onto the main road to walk into Arca. The view leading up to the hostel, Arco-O Pina, was special; across a meadow of daisies, purple pulmonaria (lungwort) and silvery grasses with pine and eucalyptus in the background.

Carolyn was an authority on the Latin names for plants. Barbara followed her around, recording these long names in her journal. It reminded me of an American horticulturalist I once met. He stated he disliked lecturing in England, as the English always knew more about gardening than he did.

The newly built hostel was a traditional design of stone and pine.

We met Richard and Russ, who had decided to keep on going to Santiago; they hoped to take a flight out tomorrow. We said our farewells. The Australian girl and her English boyfriend arrived, having also walked every inch of the way from St Jean Pied-De-Port, and I recognized other faces we had seen on the path, including a man from Spa in Belgium. Everyone embraced and exchanged anecdotes of their adventures en route.

There was a shop next to the hostel and we prepared our last picnic supper: pâté, ham, cheese, salad, fruit, crusty bread and wine. We shared one of the tables in the dining room with the middle-aged Belgian from Spa. He was eating a tin of sardines, dipping his bread into the oil. We asked if he would like to help himself to our feast. He refused at first, but when we started on our big bowl of fruit salad, with cherries, strawberries and cream, he accepted with joy. Carolyn handed our leftovers to a lively group of youngsters at another table who appeared to be eating sparsely. Everything disappeared in a flash!

There was an air of excitement at the hostel, knowing tomorrow that we would reach Santiago. There was nothing in Arca for us to see, as it was a small main road village. We rinsed our underwear and enjoyed the good bathroom facilities. Grouped together in the courtyard, warmed by the evening sun, we reminisced, chuckled and laughed over Camino memories. We were in our bunks and sound asleep by 8.00 p.m.

Thursday 7th June
SANTIAGO

We were up at 4.30 a.m. It was dark when we left. All the pilgrims at the hostel had the same idea as us: to get to Santiago before noon. There was a consultation on the *refugio* steps as we hauled on our rucksacks. The Camino path was supposedly overgrown and ran through forest for 3 km. It was pitch black and we didn't have a torch. Most of the pilgrims chose to take the main road and join the route at Amenal. At dawn, in thick mist, we took the rocky uphill path through eucalyptus and pine. At one point we walked through an area that looked just like Glen Helen in the Isle of Man. We stopped for breakfast at San Paio, a busy café full of pilgrims. It was a long wait to be served with toast and coffee. We took advantage of their bathroom, hot water, scented soap and soft towels. The café was warm and cosy; I almost dozed off in the close, heated air. When we finally got a table it was tough to get up and begin walking again.

We trudged over patches of wild mint, which smelled strongly in the damp air. We passed hedgerows with evening primrose and yellow daisies that gave a golden glow to the dull dawn. The sun was trying to peep through as we came to Labacolla.

We made our way down to the river in the mist and followed the N544 into Santiago. A massive yellow stone road sign carved with shells and crosses greeted us as we rounded the corner; we had reached Santiago! We hugged each other and collapsed in a heap around the sign after snapping photos of everyone grinning in triumph. Draped around the stone, we braced ourselves for the kilometres of suburbia to follow.

Labacolla, named after the river, is now famous for its airport, but in Picaud's time, he had this to say in his guide:

> ...and there is a river called Lauamentula; because in a leafy spot along its course two miles from Santiago French pilgrims on their way to Santiago take off their clothes and, for love of the Apostle, wash not only their private parts, but the dirt from their entire bodies... (Lozano, 1999)

We came to the village of San Marcos near the summit of Monte del Gozo and we could now see the city of Santiago in the distance. Mount Gozo houses an enormous pilgrim complex with 800 free beds; there is a campsite, auditorium and the European Pilgrimage Centre. Pilgrims were flocking onto the Camino from the complex and there was now a trail of gaunt backpackers heading toward the city. We had 4 km to walk. I found these last few kilometres the hardest; I could barely lift my feet and shuffled along, bending my knees to relieve the weight of the rucksack on my back. I felt the pressure from everyone to arrive in time for the service.

The route into the city was crowded with commuters on their way to work and children on their way to school. The local authorities had torn up part of the pavement for water main repairs and we were forced to walk in the road.

The sun shone as we entered the city and the church bells were ringing. Nothing could compare with the immense emotion and awesome feeling that swept over me as I entered through the great gate to the Plaza de Cervantes and then into the echoing plaza itself with the massive cathedral in front of us – Plaza del Obradoiro.

The square was filled with pilgrims, tourists, street vendors and musicians; the atmosphere was electric. We saw pilgrims we had met and passed en route. We embraced like long-lost friends. We went straight to the cathedral; it was packed, every seat taken. The service was about to start. We decided there were too many people and we should perhaps try to do this earlier tomorrow.

We were leaving the cathedral by the great elaborately sculpted doorway dating back to 1188, when a Spanish lady tapped me on the shoulder. 'You are not staying to see the great *botafumeiro*?' she said; 'It is a rare happening; only for something special...' I looked blank and she continued, 'the great bell pulling...'

We turned and pushed our way back inside to the central aisle. A smartly dressed middle-aged Spanish lady was reading from the altar steps. When she finished, she came to the side of the aisle where I was standing and motioned for me to take off my rucksack! Relieved, I quietly slipped the bag off my back and watched in awe as this amazing ceremony began.

It had been announced that a special gift had been received from the church in Germany and the *botafumeiro* (smoke belcher), a giant incense burner, would be used today in appreciation. This censer had for centuries sweetened the air and dispensed of the rank odour of pilgrim! Nowadays the incense was burned on St James Day (July 25th) and special feast days. The German gift, we understood later, was money! The censer was enormous: at least 4 ft high and very wide at the base. A huge thick cable descended from the dome and eight men in long red robes attached it to the burner. Lesser ropes were attached to the base and they hauled in unison, swinging the burner high up above the cathedral floor, back and forth from one transept to the other. After several pulls, the censer reached the apex of its swing, air whistled by and clouds of incense poured from the apertures in its silver casing. The swings gradually diminished and the eight men slowed the censer and pulled it to a halt, struggling as though they restrained a bucking horse.

The altar was very ornate with a statue of St James above the rich decorations. After the service we lined up with the other pilgrims and mounted the stairs behind the altar to reach forward and touch the brass cockleshell on the back of the jewelled statue. In a massive silver casket, in a crypt under the altar, are the remains of St James, minus one hand, which, legend states, was taken to England by Empress Matilda, daughter of Henry I. This was placed in a shrine at the Abbey of Reading, which was the centre of the cult of St James at that time.

Framed by the Plaza do Obradoiro, opposite the cathedral, is the formidable Gothic building, Hostal de los Reyes Catolicos, now a Parador, said to be the oldest hotel and the most emblematic in the world. A former pilgrim hospice, it has an impressive interior, full of art treasures and four cloisters of immense beauty, similar to the Parador of Leon.

We were greeted warmly as we arrived. I was expected and immediately handed a lengthy fax from the Manx Wildlife Trust. They had sent the local newspaper write-ups with a picture of me leaving the Isle of Man. The parcel I had mailed to myself was waiting with clean clothes to wear home, and a letter, from Felicity at The Trust, which contained the Manx flag to fly with all the others in the Square. Suddenly all the weariness disappeared and I seemed to have a new lease of life!

Our rooms were sumptuous, with a little balcony overlooking a leafy side street. Months ago, we had booked very expensive rooms, with three beds in each – this was a pricey hotel. Carolyn, Penny and Gwyneth sat in their room, horrified to think that one night's stay would cost more than all our hostels and *refugios* put together! I felt the unique atmosphere was worth every penny. After a shower in the palatial bathroom, I donned my Walking for Wildlife T-shirt. Ann tied my Manx flag to her walking stick and we headed out into the Square.

We stopped to take pictures by the fountain and made our way to the Casa del Dean (the Dean's house) at the rear of the cathedral to have our *credencials* (pilgrim passport) certified as proof of our journey's completion. Oddly, the office was filled with hats piled on top of bookshelves, stacked in corners and lying on chairs. They had been forgotten by pilgrims hurrying to leave.

A handsome young male assistant greeted me. I produced my passport and explained that when I began the journey I had not realized that I needed to have my passport stamped at every port of call; at Pamplona I fell asleep, too tired to go to the *refugio* office. After that I had paid attention to the stamping requirement.

It was difficult to explain the location of the Isle of Man. They were intrigued with the flag, and finally understood that it is a separate country. The handsome assistant took out the record book and entered my details for tomorrow's service. With a flourish, he thumbed through his Latin book of names to find Jean Ann and wrote out the official certificate. The clerk told us we could get folders or tubes from the stationers across the street to carry our certificates. We were now entitled to three free meals for three days at the Hotel de los Reyes Catolicos (the Parador). This is a continuation of the tradition of hospitality to pilgrims dating back to its origins as a pilgrim hospital. The Parador only serves ten free meals a day now and one ate in the Parador garage down the hill, past security and through the back door. We didn't want to do this. We felt like heroes, not beggars.

We had eaten lunch in a side street café in the overbearing shadow of the great cathedral tower. Barbara found a pension room for Friday night, as her flight did not leave until Saturday.

Ann and I bought books (*A day in Santiago de Compostela*) and went back to the Parador to put up our feet and read. Our flight was not due till late in the afternoon on Friday and we would have time to do some more sightseeing in the morning.

After a rest, we went out in the early evening to find a restaurant for our last meal together. We stopped to listen to a brass band performing in a square. The father of a little Spanish *nina* was playing in the band and she stole the show by dancing to the music, despite mummy continually dragging her back into the crowd.

Restaurants were busy and the Spanish bars and cafés full of pilgrims. I still carried the Manx flag and wore my Walking for Wildlife T-shirt, which instigated some curious looks. We chose a nice-looking Italian restaurant, which wasn't very patriotic for our last night, but we had an urge for pasta! I propped my flag in the flowerpot adjacent to my seat and settled down to an enjoyable meal with lots of wine and laughter. The day had covered so much; it seemed like a dream. Light-headed and weary, we wended our way back to the comfort of a night at the Parador.

Friday 8th June
SANTIAGO TO HEATHROW

We had a good breakfast at the Parador to see us through the morning, then took our backpacks to the reception desk, ready for the afternoon departure. At 10.00 a.m. the plaza began to fill up with vendors and entertainers ready to greet and fleece the pilgrims of the day.

Plaza Obradoiro took its name from the *obradores*, or stonemasons' workshops, situated in the square during the long period of the cathedral's construction. Ann and I went back to the cathedral for another look at the Portico de la Gloria (Doorway to Glory). The portico is renowned for the lifelike figures carved into and around the three arches of the doorway. Master Mateo supervised the carving, which was accomplished mainly between the years 1168–1188:

> Maestro Mateo's self-awareness as an artist is unusual for the Romanesque period. After securing the King's and the Cathedral Council's explicit permission, with pride he sculpted himself on the base of the parteluz in the guise of a kneeling worshiper looking toward the distant high altar. Today stressed-out students clunk their heads against this kneeling figure, the Santo dos Croques, to ensure success on their examinations. (Gitlitz and Davidson, 2000:354)

There are more than 200 sculptured figures in realistic poses distributed amongst the three arches of the doorway that lead to the aisles. The central column was one of the reasons Ann and I had returned. We wanted to see the carving known as the Tree of Jesse (Christ's family tree), above which sits St James, serenely smiling to welcome the exhausted pilgrims. It is traditional for each pilgrim to place his hands upon the 'tree' and pray with thankfulness for his safe arrival. Over a thousand years of pilgrim hands have worn deep grooves into the carven stone. The perspiration and oil from these hands has refined the stone into a satin marble surface. We set our hands on the cold marble, bowed our heads and prayed in penitence and gratitude.

Johann, an Austrian priest, was standing behind us. We had seen him many times on the route. He introduced us to his wife and sister, who had flown out to join him on his arrival in Santiago. They had family in Florida and were eager to talk with Ann. I asked where they came from in Austria. Remarkably, Johann was the priest at the Frauenkirchen Ann and I had visited when walking in Austria over forty years ago. I promised to send him an old black and white photograph, if I could find it. His wife's sister took a photograph of us. It was very moving.

It rained, our first for a fortnight. We made our way to the Plaza de la Azabacheria facing the north façade of the cathedral. Penny was fascinated by the silver and jet trinkets in the jewellery stores and booths surrounding this area of the cathedral. For 700 years artisans have carved jet souvenirs, scallop shells, beads and religious symbols for acquisitive pilgrims; after all, *azabache* means jet in Spanish. Claude from France walked by, half-shrouded by a large umbrella. He looked as pristine as ever in a fresh white T-shirt. He had walked in today and was en route to the Mass. It seemed that Richard and Russ were finally ahead of him!

Back at the cathedral the Mass was held and the list of pilgrims and their place of origin was read from the altar. This honoured all who had arrived on foot the previous day. I felt completely moved to hear *Uno ila de Manos*. I clutched in my hand the remaining half of my scallop shell, which I had carried from the Isle of Man. With tears in my eyes, I walked out into the rain and tossed the shell into the pilgrim fountain.

We returned to the Parador for our farewells.

The taxis were booked and ready to leave. Barbara strode away across the square, her scallop shell that signified her pilgrim status dangling from her rucksack. Full of emotion, we watched her go. The rain trickled down the cab windows and our eyes blurred with tears as we sped to the airport.

Walk in 2002
BACK TO THE CAMINO

When we rode across the Sierras in John's camper van, we were disappointed by the lost opportunity to backpack through the region. Because our flights had been booked from Santiago, we could not take the extra days needed for the mountains.

I looked at Ann as she gazed in frustration through the window. 'Yes,' I said, 'I will see Samos and O Cebreiro. I swear I'll complete the route.'

Ann turned to me. 'Okay, next year Samos!' she said firmly.

Friday 30th August
VILLAFRANCA DEL BIERZO TO SAMOS AND TRIACASTELLA

Ann and I had taken the overnight ferry to Santander and driven down to Villafranca. We were at the Parador de Villa Franca del Bierzo; a splendid luxurious change from last year's stay at the refuge. Martin, the handsome young Spanish receptionist, had promised to keep the car safely in the staff parking lot while we hiked the mountains.

At breakfast we continued discussing our route. We had booked a taxi for 9.00am, but remained undecided about the most appropriate itinerary.

At last, an impulsive decision: 'We can take the taxi to Samos and walk back to the car at Villafranca.'

The bemused Martin listened to our twittering tizzy and wasn't sure where the dithering old ladies were going!

We arrived at the monastery of Samos, a huge edifice, obviously once a wealthy Catholic bastion against the Moors; so wealthy that it had been attacked three times by pirates.

A cheery, chunky monk stood at the entrance, whittling a stick in a notched pattern. He told us the monastery would be open in ten minutes.

A young Spanish girl conducted the guided tour. Her limited English was indecipherable. The German pilgrims who accompanied us were baffled. I struggled to translate both ways: Spanish/English, English/German with limited success.

We were shown the oldest doorway in the building. The frame was composed of Roman columns and a headstone of Celtic origin had been added in the fifth-century. Nearby we saw the fountain of the Nereids, young, full-breasted nymphs.

Very erotic for a monastery. An enormous palm tree in the courtyard gave the place an exotic Moorish feel, towering over the monument of San Benito (1676–1764). This saint, who excelled at his studies, was the author of the first encyclopedias and eventually chaired several Spanish universities.

Most of the abbey was destroyed by fire in 1537, and rebuilding continued through the centuries whenever funding became available. Tragically, in 1951, a massive fire devastated the refectory and the library.

A modern mural, painted in three styles by Madrid University art students, encircled the second story colonnade. Interestingly, the faces of the monks were contemporary brothers and well known present-day personalities.

Within the church near the altar was the small statue of a pilgrim. He wore a bright red cloak swathed around his waist and hips, a jaunty hat and a cheerful smile, more reminiscent of a cavalier than the tattered, dusty pilgrim depicted at most shrines. A candle burned before him. Pilgrims have been welcomed to this monastery since the eleventh-century.

The town of Samos consisted mainly of the monastery, a café/bar and a petrol station. The café/bar was a startling transition from the hallowed monastic atmosphere. A Madonna video blasted forth, closely watched by the lounging locals.

We began the reverse trip to Triacastella by walking a kilometre along the main road, dodging lorries and vicious Spanish cars. We descended at last to the pilgrim track along the river, through several small hamlets. Stone-built tumbledown houses lined muddy, manure-strewn streets. The houses were roofed with large blue slates circled like pancakes over the beams. Spare tiles were stacked vertically in boxes like plates in a rack, alongside the road, ready for replacing roof tiles in the harsh winter storms. A flock of sheep escaped the burning midday sun by huddling under a derelict lean-to by the river.

The farmyards burst with flowers; all the manure, I suppose. Hollyhocks towered over our heads. There were dahlias as large as saucers: bright orange, red and purple. Corn as high as the proverbial elephant's eye. Resting against the stone walls were wheels, old stone mill wheels, worn and grooved. Cartwheels in the traditional Galician style formed like buttons: huge, solid wooden circles with a hole in the middle for the axle.

We passed medieval barns with sagging beams and crumbling walls, which sometimes housed gleaming modern farm equipment.

After 8 km of uphill walking beneath shady trees, the route merged with the main road. Still ascending in blistering heat, we constantly leapt onto the verge as the traffic pounded by. The traffic fumes mingled with the smell of mint, crushed by our feet as we cowered in the wayside scrub. We were blessed to pass a stream of running water piped into a basin, where pilgrims could rest and drink their fill. We took off our boots and held our burning feet under the flowing spout.

Terrified by the dangerous pilgrim route leading from Triacastella, we were thankful to have unravelled the mystery of the yellow arrows. Because we were walking the Camino in reverse, the painted yellow arrows that indicated turns in the road ahead appeared to us after we committed to the turn which caused us to hesitate and cast about like hounds circling for the scent.

We arrived in the town square at 4.30 p.m. and stopped for a cold drink in the nearest bar. Six old men were huddled around a table playing cards. Cigarettes drooped and ashes flew as they argued. Their voices rose and the beer bottles rattled as they thumped the table. Showdown at the old folks' corral! We were fascinated by the angry bursts of Spanish. Finally, the proprietor stepped in and moved to confiscate the cards. Like chastised children, their voices subsided. They sat down and resumed play.

We stayed at the nearest *albergue* (lodging house), too exhausted to find the *refugio*. Nonetheless, we had to climb three flights of stairs to our room. The lumpy pillows were a pilgrim penance, macerated foam rubber wrapped in sacking.

Triacastella was a thriving small cosmopolitan town. Bars and restaurants filled with pilgrims. We ate dinner sheltered by a striped canopy in a street of outdoor cafés.

Saturday 31st August
TRIACASTELLA TO ALTO DE POIO

Down three flights of stairs, our sticks and boots rattled on every step. Breakfast of toast, marmalade and coffee in the bar. We met three male walkers from Birmingham, their legs covered with scratches, welts and bruises. They stated a preference for going over the mountains rather than following the paths. Typical Brits! One must suffer to enjoy oneself.

We walked out of town and found the dusty Camino grinding uphill. Families labouring in the fields waved to us. '*Vuelta,*' (turn round) they called, nodding their heads. 'No, Santiago – you are going the wrong way!'

'Villafranca, Villafranca,' we shouted and gestured in return, appreciating their helpfulness.

Harebells and daisies nodded in the hedgerows. Patchwork fields blanketed the slopes, each field enclosed by brambly hedges and fences. Obviously, there was more subsistence from farming than large-scale agriculture. There were gentle brown cows everywhere, herded by women, boys and dogs. Men must work the farm machinery, or have other jobs in nearby towns. Some of the younger women had dyed their hair red. It glowed fluorescently in the morning sun. Was this a new fashion? Dark Spanish hair did not dye to a lighter colour.

Little mud-encrusted cars chugged up and down the roads. The villages of Ramil and Fonfria were still medieval in character, with heavily beamed floors, the supporting beams protruding through old stone walls. The farmhouses had byres beneath, manure piled high, with flies swarming around. At Ramil, in the centre of the village square surrounded by stone houses and arched doorways, was a massive beech tree with several trunks melded into one. Small, gnarled branches protruded from the trunk like errant hairs in an old man's eyebrow. It could have been a scene from the 1700s.

Maize and corn waved in the breeze and the smell of cabbages mingled with the sour odour of dairy and cowpats. This faded as we rose higher to hedgerows of heather and gorse dying in the late summer sun. Trees were smaller and bent to the direction of the wind at the higher altitude. Young trees had been planted in rows alongside the pilgrim road. Marker stones decorated with the shell symbol were placed with Lugo efficiency every half kilometre, which heartened us as we pressed upwards.

We came unstuck where the Camino crossed the road at Filloval; there were no yellow arrows and we had to backtrack. It was good to rest for a while in a derelict bus shelter surrounded by nettles and a rusting Filloval sign. At least we knew where we were.

At Biduelo there was a little restaurant and hostel, clean and newly painted, with slabs of tree trunk as seats and tables on an overgrown patch of lawn. A walker lay asleep in the long grass. Another barefoot pilgrim arrived. His girlfriend helped him limp to a table, obviously depleted from the climb to O Cebreiro and the walk down. We met a New Zealander and an Aussie girl, heady with their triumphant walk so far. They told us that the road was sometimes uphill, then flat, and occasionally a short stretch down. It was encouraging, as other pilgrims had indicated that the road was very steep, almost vertical in places. One of the girls showed us her arms, covered in little red bites from the fleas she had picked up in a refuge in Villafranca. Perhaps it was the refuge we stayed in last year where we saw rats. I didn't want to stay in a refuge with fleas – rat fleas carry the plague.

The afternoon was hot and we rose higher and higher. Triacastella was now way below us, a misty dot. Onwards and up to Alto del Poio, 1337 metres. An exhausting haul. In the distance we could see this remote point on the Camino. A bus surrounded by cyclists was parked in front of the hostel. Fear gripped me. We could be out of luck; no room at the inn. But God heard my fervent prayer. The bus pulled away and the cyclists sped down the hill.

At the top of the pass was a simple hostel with hot showers and comfortable beds. Laundry completed, we hung it out to dry on a balcony line above the hostel yard, where an Alsation slept under a rusted road sign. Ann's freshly washed knickers fell off the line, plonk, into the dog's pen. He snarled up at us. We asked the proprietor to retrieve them. I don't know who was the most embarrassed, the proprietor, the dog or Ann!

> During the day you won't see wolves along here, but you may spot their droppings along the trail. In the eighteenth-century, pilgrims feared bandits in these wild and foggy forests. The Italian pilgrim Albani noted seeing small crosses stuck in the ground where travellers had been robbed or murdered. (Gitlitz and Davidson, 2000:308)

The wolves could be the reason for the large numbers of ferocious guard dogs kept in the farms we passed on the way.

The sun set and the air chilled. A log fire blazed in the stone hearth of the hostel bar, a welcome end to the day.

Sunday 1st September
ALTO DE POIO TO HERREIRAS

We slept badly after a late meal of fatty pork chops. Not our choice, but all that was available.

Early morning at Alto do Poia, the mist shrouded the valleys with a cold wind; the sun was glimmering redly on the hills. Ann had been awakened before dawn by the sound of hikers leaving the hostel across the road. She said their shapes against the light looked like hooded dwarves, hunched over by the heavy packs on their backs.

We walked along the high road, swept by the chilly gusts that swirled around the cliffs. At Alto San Roque we took photos of the bronze statue of Santiago, bent against the gales struggling along the mountain top road. Hikers came down the hill, shivering and pale. The views of the mountains spread out for miles. It was spectacular.

At Hospital da Condesa we met a striking figure in a sweatshirt blazoned with Santiago Compostela, on his head a blue turban secured by a cord and a large scallop shell. He was a grizzled British guy on his third segment of the Camino. He started in March, returning in May to get as far as Logrono and now back to complete the route. In the meantime he had set up a web site for like-minded individuals to make contact with news from the Camino.

The route continued down through Linares with banks of sweet-smelling pinky mauve wild carnations and crops of wild crocus. A flower I associated with springtime glinted through the autumn grass on the hill. What a surprise. A polecat leapt away in fright as we took photographs.

O Cebreiro at last, snuggled into the hillside, crowded with tourists, cars and Spanish families rushing to the church for morning service. The sanctuary was built of stone, similar to a Cotswold stone wall, very small, with a bell tower which did not protrude much above the hills because of the wind. There were postcards of the church covered with snow. The winters must be ferocious up here. Several refuges and hostels were doing a roaring trade on this now sunny day.

We looked at an old Galician house, a rondel with a thatched roof. Inside the hut, which appeared surprisingly spacious, the fireplace was encircled by wooden benches. Blackened hoops of wood were hung from the ceiling where flitches and other meat were smoked to preserve them through the winter. A small half-door separated the sleeping quarters from the cooking area. A rickety wooden bedstead and a hand carved cradle were in the bedroom. The shelves in the eating area held an assortment of handmade wooden platters. It was surprising to me that wood was utilized in so many ways as the large trees grew so much lower on the slopes.

The steep dusty track out of the village continued to take us down on rough stone through the magnificent countryside and quiet rural hamlets. Pilgrim feet over the centuries had worn the path down between the banks, sometimes as high as four feet on the sides. Vegetation on the side of the path had begun to brown into autumn. Errant ears of wheat rustled and drooped in the sun.

We stopped at a bar in La Farba for lunch. For one euro I had a big bowl of chicken soup with pasta. Peseta coins had this year been replaced by bright new shiny euros.

With renewed energy we tackled the precipitous worn rocky path from La Farba, which would have been impossible to ascend in rainy weather. Clouds of dust floated up around us and coated our clothes and hair in ochre powder. It was now very hot and the tar melted by the side of the road. We stopped by the River Valcarce. There was a spring piped from the river; it gushed through a stone wall. I stood under the spray, letting it rush over my bare feet. The stone benches nearby were sheltered by a spreading tree.

I leaned back and dozed, while Ann lay on the wall in the shade. An old man interrupted our siesta, delighted to practice his broken English. A family, grandparents, daughter and granddaughter, strolled by and joined us. We were polite to them and smiled and chatted, attempting to understand each other. I would have preferred to doze in the sun as I dreaded the kilometres ahead.

We still had a long way to go to Vega de Valcarce, where there was a hostel. Ann and I walked wearily uphill to Herreiras. I spotted a large, new rustic tourist restaurant and hotel set above the river. It was a joy to get off the road. A haven at last.

Monday 2nd September
HERREIRAS TO VILLAFRANCA DEL BIERZO

We left Las Herreiras after the usual *tostado* and *marmelada* breakfast. We were mystified by our morning experience.

As we picked up our backpacks and locked the bedroom door, an angry little Spanish woman burst out of the next room. She screamed, 'You have been keeping me awake for hours by your talking. I cannot stand you people.'

As we had arisen at 7.00 a.m. and it was now 8.30, this was a wild exaggeration. Besides, Ann and I are very reserved English women who speak in well-modulated tones!

We began the path from Herreiras, slightly uphill, dusty and roughly surfaced. It was very quiet. We could follow the boot prints of our fellow pilgrims easily. The Valcarce river was a gurgling accompaniment most of the way. Before long we came to Vega de Valcarce, a prosperous little town.

There were many people waiting in a queue for a bus to the city. I didn't envy them. It was such a beautiful day, sun shining, flowers everywhere: dahlias, hydrangeas and roses blossoming. There were also hanging baskets of petunias and nasturtiums. The town appeared colourful and prosperous. What a lovely place to grow up, I thought, a little town nestled by the river, sheltered by the swaying trees and the hills beyond, but within the reach of several large cities. To our joy, just beyond the bus stop, was a bank with a cash point. We had been broke for a couple of days.

The cowbells clonked as we walked along. Little brown calves gambolled in the meadow grass by their solemnly munching mothers. A muddy pen of bull calves was outside the town; no soft grass, swaying trees or peaceful river for them. The poor creatures were bunched together, obviously waiting to be sent to market.

The A6 rumbled overhead, concrete piers supporting the highway vaulting across the valley. The towns could live in peace: no articulated lorries pounded by their homes, cracking their walls and loosening the roof tiles. No screeching brakes and grinding gears constantly accompanied their daily lives. The NV1 was now 'the old road'.

We pushed on to Trabadelo. The chorus of helpful farmers followed us. 'You are going the wrong way!'

A Guardia Civil van stopped to inquire our destination. They were handsome black-eyed Spanish police in tight-fitting uniforms (I was a pushover for a uniform in my youth). I felt tempted to turn around and walk the 'right' way to Santiago for their sake!

Many of the fields we passed had crops of cabbages and beans, wilting in the unusual heat.

The churches we saw had two small stone arches built onto a peak at one end. The arches were surmounted by a cross and within each arch a small bell was suspended.

The wide valley of the Valcarce was topped by a ruined castle on the mountain overlooking the town. Originally the bastion of the Sarracin family, whose retainers marauded throughout the countryside, robbing and killing any pilgrims who refused to pay their toll. The designated pilgrim way was along the NV1, much quieter than previous years, now that the new road was finished. Nevertheless, we struggled along the rock-strewn path on the far side of the steel barrier, hoping cars wouldn't swerve into us as we sidled over the bridges.

We stopped at Trabadelo for lunch, a *bocadillo* composed of a four-egg potato omelette nestled in a loaf of crusty bread. Thus fortified, we walked onwards. A dapper little man on a bicycle advised us against taking the upper road over the hills (as our book suggested) because it was a steep climb. The road was not busy now and much faster by several kilometres.

Pilgrims reeled by on their way from Villafranca, facing the tortuous 2 km climb up to La Farba at the end of their day. Pereje was abandoned along the NV1. Houses were tumbling into decay, but as we walked up the hill away from the main road, the village brightened: new paint, flowering windowboxes, comfortable benches for families to rest in the afternoon sun. Rows of little white houses swarmed up the slope and the village seemed joyous to have escaped the busy road.

We arrived in Villafranca at teatime. The last obstacle was a fearsome dark tunnel. I could not believe this was the way into the town. An elderly couple, silhouetted against the light at the far end of the tunnel, boldly strode through, carrying fishing gear.

'Is there another way into town?' I asked.

They looked at me in amazement. 'This is safe,' they chorused. 'No cars, see, no cars.'

We stumbled along, hugging the right side of the squalid tunnel and passed workmen returning home. The tunnel dripped and water gurgled in the gutter.

We walked up the hill to the Parador and collapsed in chairs.

'Afternoon tea,' we croaked, through dusty throats, to the beaming Martin, who assured us the car was safe.

Revived, I decided to heave our rucksacks into the car and take the long, narrow winding road back to O Cebreiro. We spent the night in a newly built *albergue* (lodging house), with comfortable beds, an en suite bathroom, and fresh mountain air streaming through the windows. The night was chilly and as usual all the pilgrims retired early, to begin the next day's trek at dawn.

Tuesday 3rd September
O CEBREIRO

Dogs barked intermittently throughout the night. Cows rustled in the byre opposite our open window. As the hikers assembled at dawn, a calf scrambled through the byre door, followed by his anxious mother. Hikers abruptly scattered and a dog sprang nose to nose with the cow and barked ferociously. The cow backed away. Maybe these insomniac guard dogs were useful. The hikers certainly began their walk at record speed.

Lightning flared behind the nearby mountains, thunder rumbled around and echoed in the valley.

'Is that blasting from the quarry?' Ann called.

'I don't think so, the electricity just went off.'

No delicious machine-ground percolated coffee for breakfast, only milky *descafeinados* (decaffeinated) and hunks of bread with *marmelada*, which we ate in the twilight of the bar.

Thunder and lightning continued as we walked to the church. The roof was being repaired, the workmen ignored the storm, perched upon the tiles hammering and sawing. They were rushing to finish before the annual celebration on September 8th, when 30,000 people converge on the church to celebrate Mass and commemorate the miracle of the communion vessels, which happened in the thirteenth-century. A devout peasant from Barxamaior had stumbled through snowdrifts to celebrate mass at the little church. The priest, probably cold and cranky, scoffed at the poor man for coming through such a snowstorm for bread and wine. The bread and wine were transformed into flesh and blood as he spoke. This miracle was affirmed by the Pope in 1487, and has been celebrated ever since.

The painted statue of the Virgin holding the Child, her head bowed, her enamelled wooden smile beneficently gazed down at the empty nave. I noticed she was chained to the wall for safety. We lighted candles in gratitude for the blessings we had received in making our way through the mountains and for the continued well-being of everyone we had left at home. It was the end of our Camino walk. We had completed the final miles. A memorable trip of a lifetime.

Biographies

JEAN

Jean had spent thirty years running a successful recruitment and secretarial agency in Kent and dreamed happily of retirement days ahead with husband, Clifford. The 1980s had been an emotional and difficult time. She had watched her father die of cancer and went on to nurse her terminally ill mother. 1990 was to be the golden year of her life with her devoted Cliff. They planned to spend four months of each year in the new home they had built in the mountains of Southern Spain. But, sadly, that was not to be: in March 1990, he, too, died of cancer.

Her son, Stuart, and daughter, Lynda, tried to comfort her in her loss, but Jean sought to make a new beginning. Relocating to the Isle of Man afforded Jean the opportunity to expand a lifelong interest in wildlife and conservation, working as a project and volunteer coordinator for the Manx Wildlife Trust. When her friend Ann visited the island with her sisters, Caroline and Penny, to walk the island's Route of the Gull, a decision was made for a walk together to celebrate the new millennium along the Camino to Santiago de Compostela. This triggered off the idea to make the most of her efforts by seeking sponsorship for her walk to help support the work of the Manx Wildlife Trust, its twenty nature reserves and two visitor centres.

At sixty-five, Jean had had a share of misfortune in her life in the form of a broken first marriage and then in her prime, survived both cervical and colon cancer.

Despite all the stress of these years, Jean's new life on the Isle of Man had given her inner strength and the walk was to be her personal pilgrimage of thanks for her life, her family, her work and especially her four grandchildren, who are very dear to her.

Jean returned to the peace of her island home a stone in weight lighter, minus two big toenails and nursing very sore feet, but her spirits rose high when she was welcomed with the news that she had raised nearly £3,000 for the Manx Wildlife Trust.

ANN

Ann has endured difficult years. Surgical operations included a colostomy and a lumpectomy. During radiation, et cetera, Ann had nursed her mother-in-law through the final stages of Alzheimer's and coped with her husband and his battle with clinical depression. Finally, after grandma's death, Ann began to assess her own life. 'Mostly just kept the grindstone going!' she thought. Dreams had shattered or become meaningless as the years piled up.

As a teenager, Ann helped raise her younger sisters after her mother's death. A couple of years of travel in Europe followed by early marriage to an American and the birth of two daughters had driven the wanderlust underground. 'I still leapt to attention at the sight of a travel brochure!' she said. While working full time, Ann had obtained her masters degree in social work, and for some years worked in an adolescent psychiatric unit.

The children were grown and the grandchildren had arrived. Ann remembered her dreams of travel. Walking on the beach in Florida, near her home, the scattered shells reminded her of the scallop shell, the pilgrim emblem from Santiago. 'I wanted to walk the pilgrim trail as a child; it seemed a romantic adventure. Now it is more than an adventure, it can be a trip of thankfulness and prayer. I am a cancer survivor, my family are growing in their own lives, and my husband is recovering. I'll walk the trail and thank God for the blessings He has given me as well as the hope for a better future.'

When Ann spoke to Jean, she thought it was a great idea and the planning began. They aimed for a millennium walk. But when Ann broke her foot the trip was postponed for a year. Nevertheless, in May 2001, they started their journey.

BARBARA

Jean and Barbara were working colleagues at Doubleday publishers in New York in the late 50s. Barbara was in foreign and reprint rights and Jean was in international sales.

Barbara married Alan, a US diplomat. They travelled the world on long-term assignments (Rotterdam, Kuala Lumpur, Seoul, Papua New Guinea and Moscow). Their daughter, Beth, was born in Malaysia, and they spent five years at the US embassy in Seoul, where their son, Alex, was born.

After Barbara volunteered at an orphanage there, they adopted a brother and sister, seven and three years old. Two years later, they found and adopted the Korean children's long-lost sister. Suddenly they had five children! Beth was not a well child and demanded a lot of Barbara's time. Managing a large family and spending years abroad was sometimes exhausting.

When Alan retired, Barbara carried on working full time, even after she became ill with breast cancer. An added blow was the death of their dear adopted son, Steve, who was killed in a road accident on Christmas Eve 1993. The family was shattered.

Barbara, like Jean and Ann, is a survivor, and when she read of their pilgrim walk in Jean's millennium letter, she emailed immediately and said, 'Can I come, too?'

CAROLYN

Carolyn had nursed her father until his death at the age of ninety-two. She worked full time and raised three children, a son and two daughters. Carolyn had four grandchildren. Her youngest daughter had been seriously ill a couple of years before, but was now doing well. As children, all the sisters had hiked for miles with their parents through the countryside. All four girls, Judith, Ann, Carolyn and Penny had learned to love walking. When Ann suggested the Camino trail as a way of expressing their gratitude for life's blessings, the girls jumped at the chance.

PENNY

The youngest sister in the group, at the age of fifty-four. Penny had spent her life in the Cotswolds, raising two boys. Penny, an accomplished painter and weaver, spent part of her days teaching art to disabled people, and also creating magnificent wall hangings.

Penny's eldest son had a severe motorcycle accident, from which he recovered. But Penny also felt a need to make the walk in gratitude.

GWYNETH

Gwyneth was a close friend of Penny's. She worked full time, managing a Citizens Advice Bureau, and had two grown children. Recently separated from her husband, Gwyneth looked upon the trip as an opportunity to begin her life as an independent woman.

Bibliography of Works Cited

Bishton, Derek, 'Back from the Future', *Daily Telegraph* (UK), Saturday 22 April 2000.

Gitlitz, David M. and Davidson, Linda Kaye, *The Pilgrimage Road to Santiago*, New York, St Martins Press.

Hopkins, Adam, Daily Telegraph Travel, Weekend Telegraph, 21 June 1997.

Lozano, Bravo Millan, *A Practical Guide for Pilgrims*, Editorial Everest, 6th edn. 1999.

Confraternity of St. James[*]; *Pilgrim Guides to Spain*, The Camino Frances, 2001 (updated annually).

---

[*]27 Blackfriars Road, London SE1 8NY, www.csj.org.uk

Printed in the United Kingdom
by Lightning Source UK Ltd.
102021UKS00001B/283-312